Improving Student Learning: Action Principles for Families, Classrooms, Schools, Districts, and States

Improving Student Learning: Action Principles for Families, Classrooms, Schools, Districts, and States

Herbert J. Walberg

http://www.centerii.org

INFORMATION AGE PUBLISHING, INC.
Charlotte, NC • www.infoagepub.com

Library of Congress Cataloging-in-Publication Data

Walberg, Herbert J., 1937-
  Improving Student Learning : action principles for families, classrooms,
schools, districts, and states / Herbert J. Walberg.
      p. cm.
  Includes bibliographical references.
  ISBN 978-1-61735-212-6 (pbk.) – ISBN 978-1-61735-213-3 (hardcover) –
ISBN 978-1-61735-214-0 (e-book)
1. School improvement programs. 2. Teacher effectiveness. 3.
Schools–Evaluation. 4. Educational evaluation. I. Title.
  LB2822.8.W25 2011
  371.2'07–dc22
                            2010038053

Printed in the United States of America

CONTENTS

ACKNOWLEDGEMENTS

The author is appreciative of the suggestions made by Sam Redding who has critiqued this book at various stages, from concept to outline to draft. I am also grateful to those who copy edited the manuscript and designed the publication: Marilyn Murphy, Stephen Page, Pamela Sheley, and Lori Thomas, as well as Michelle McFadden for the cover design.

CENTER ON INNOVATION & IMPROVEMENT

121 N. Kickapoo Street
Lincoln, IL 62656 USA
Phone: 217-732-6462
Fax: 217-732-3696

www.center.org

The Center on Innovation & Improvement is administered by the Academic Development Institute (Lincoln, IL) in collaboration with its partners, Temple University Institute for Schools and Society (Philadelphia, PA) and Little Planet Learning (Nashville, TN).

INFORMATION • TOOLS • TRAINING

Positive results for students will come from changes in the knowledge, skill, and behavior of their teachers and parents. State policies and programs must provide the opportunity, support, incentive, and expectation for adults close to the lives of children to make wise decisions.

The Center on Innovation & Improvement helps Regional Comprehensive Centers in their work with states to provide districts, schools, and families with the opportunity, information, and skills to make wise decisions on behalf of students.

A national content center supported by the U. S. Department of Education's Office of Elementary and Secondary Education.

Award #S283B050057

The opinions expressed herein do not necessarily reflect the position of the supporting agencies, and no official endorsement should be inferred.

FOREWORD

As always, my friend Herb Walberg brings to his writing the three perspectives he describes in the concluding chapter in this book—science, wisdom, and common sense. This book's intention is ambitious, weaving together the various levels of influence on student learning. Walberg opens with introductory remarks that frame the historical context and a philosophical undergirding of American schools. He proceeds from the student's own psychological prerequisites for learning to the direct contributions of the family and classroom, to the indirect contributions of the school and district, and finally the overarching systems and supports provided by the state. He leaves nothing unexamined, including the promise of technology, charter schools, performance incentives, and turnaround initiatives. Regardless of the method proposed, Walberg reminds us of the fundamental variables of time and effort, competent instruction, and consideration for the in-school and out-of-school experiences that propel each student's personal success.

Walberg is a master at proposing concrete, practical measures in layman's terms supported by the best evidence from education science. His own wisdom accumulated from a distinguished career as one of the world's leading researchers enables him to draw from the reservoirs of research literature and present it in succinct, readable form.

Improving Student Learning: Action Principles for Families, Classrooms, Schools, Districts, and States, pages xi–xii

                                        xi

The Center on Innovation & Improvement has proudly drawn upon Herb Walberg, the Center's Chief Scientific Advisor, to produce a *Handbook on Restructuring and Substantial School Improvement* and a *Handbook on State-wide Systems of Support*. Both of these publications are now found, dog-eared and underlined, in the offices of policy makers and administrators, as well as the classrooms of teachers across the country. They built the foundation for the services the Center provides its sister centers in the technical assistance network funded by the U. S. Department of Education and the network's service to state education agencies.

The Center on Innovation & Improvement is delighted that *Improving Student Learning: Action Principles for Families, Classrooms, Schools, Districts, and States* comes to publication at this critical time in education reform. The Center's recent work on school turnarounds and transformations is bolstered by Walberg's threading together of the influences on student learning and his call for us to redouble our efforts on behalf of the present and future generations of students. We will study this book, take lessons from it, and do our part to make the promise of education a reality for all students.

Sam Redding
Director, Center on Innovation & Improvement
Executive Director, Academic Development Institute

CHAPTER 1

INTRODUCTION AND PURPOSE

Parents, employers, and national, state, and local leaders are gravely concerned about the performance of American schools (Howell, West, & Peterson, 2008). Elementary and middle school students lag behind students from other economically advanced countries on achievement tests and fall further behind during the school years (Walberg, 2001). Despite substantially rising school costs in the last four decades, fewer students graduated on time from high school in 2009 than in 1970 (Walberg, 2010). American research universities rank second to none in the world, but many colleges and universities must provide remedial programs for ill-prepared high school graduates.

The public increasingly recognizes the seriousness of school problems. The 2008 *Education Next* national survey report showed that the percentage of the public that gave schools a grade of A or B declined from 30% in 2005 to just 18% in 2008 (Howell et al., 2008). These problems are even more important in a new century when high levels of knowledge and skills partially determine national prosperity and citizens' quality of life. It is no longer news that large Asian countries have improved their schools considerably. Attributable to rapid advances in manufacturing and services, national incomes in China and India have been growing at as much as three times the rate of those in Europe and the United States.

Improving Student Learning: Action Principles for Families, Classrooms, Schools, Districts, and States, pages 1–7

1

Over long time periods, rapid growth makes for huge differences in prosperity. In the early 1960s, for example, Singapore and Jamaica had about the same national income. Jamaica stuck to agriculture, mining, and tourism, while Singapore improved its education system and concentrated on skilled manufacturing and advanced technology. By 2009, Singapore's income was 7 times Jamaica's, about $39,000 per person, and higher than several European countries (Milken, 2009).

American taxpayers are also concerned for another reason. The per-person costs of education, healthcare, and other government-involved sectors are among the most costly in the world, yet the United States ranks poorly on the return on its investment. A recent survey of 30 economically advanced countries, for example, showed the United States with the fourth highest infant mortality rate, which ranked better only than Turkey, Mexico, and Slovakia (Chapple & Richardson, 2009). In the field of education, American schools scored poorly on achievement tests despite high costs per student, which are in the upper three of the 25 advanced countries participating in international achievement surveys (Walberg, 2001).

PURPOSE AND PROGRESS

In view of these valid concerns, this book summarizes the major research findings that show how to substantially increase student achievement. This book does not address the important question of content or what should be learned but the process or how achievement can be raised effectively and efficiently in the major school subjects. School boards, other elected or appointed groups, and educators are responsible for specifying the content or subject matter that schools should teach. It is their responsibility to set specifications for learning in such subjects and skills as reading, mathematics, and science. These are matters of values. Given such values and curriculum specifications, however, this book represents an effort to specify what parents, teachers, and education and state leaders can do to bring about high levels of achievement and skills in the content chosen for learning.

For at least 2,500 years, education scholarship chiefly concerned the ends and means, specifically the values of ends and the ethics of means—issues of philosophy, history, the humanities, and personal values. The more scientific question concerns the degree to which the means can efficiently bring about the ends. There seems little reason to argue about the ethics of the means; if they don't foster learning goals, more efficacious means should be chosen.

Since this book centers on the efficacy of means, it is worthwhile considering the scientific question of education causality, which rigorously arose only in the last few decades. Education science lags behind agronomy and medicine by perhaps 75 and 50 years, respectively. In agriculture, the application of scientific investigation and the promulgation of its findings produced astonishing increases in productivity such that the percentage of American farmers in the formerly agrarian population declined to less than 5% while managing to generate a surplus of food to feed citizens of the United States and other parts of the world.

Similarly, in the medical field, scientific methods of epidemiology and randomized experiments to evaluate public hygiene, new drugs, and medical procedures helped to substantially increase life spans in the United States and other parts of the world. Since scientific progress in agriculture and medicine anticipates the development of education research today, a medical example may be helpful.

In 1949, Jerry Morris was curious about rising rates of mortality attributable to heart disease (Kuper, 2009). In the study of a number of occupations, Morris noticed twice the rate of fatal heart disease among London bus drivers than conductors who climbed as many as 1000 stair steps a day on double-decker buses. Contrary to prevalent medical opinion that the cause of heart disease was exhaust fumes from the rising numbers of cars, he held that exercise may help prevent heart disease, a view that met doubt and derision.

But steadfast, Morris also observed that postal workers who delivered mail by walking or bicycling also suffered lower rates of heart disease than postal office workers. His view was repeatedly confirmed by subsequent epidemiological investigations. Even more decisively, he made comparisons of rodents and dogs that led sedentary lives with those randomly assigned for regular exercise on treadmills in what are known as experiments, the " gold currency" of causal investigations. The results showed similar differences.

APPLIED SCIENCE AND CAUSALITY

Thus, contrary to common views, scientific progress depends more on skepticism than proof. From doubt about conventional views arise new discoveries, which also deserve doubt. Even if a new idea better and more parsimoniously explains the facts, it too may be overturned by new and better evidence. For example, the theory of the balance of "the four body humors" guided medicine for centuries, and its application may have led to the deliberate bleeding of George Washington, which may have led to his death. Similarly, Galileo was persecuted for his view that challenged unanimous scholarship holding that the sun revolves around the earth.

Factual evidence is, of course, a major criterion for the validity of scientific ideas. For this reason, much of science concerns evidence and description. But much of science also concerns the question of "why," particularly applied science that seeks to change the world and thereby improve human conditions. Much of human life, of course, relies on inferences from unscientific but often useful observation. We need no scientific study of physics to know that hammers can successfully pound nails.

But human behavior, especially learning, is generally much more difficult to explain and to change. For example, skillful teachers may see in their students' faces that they understand a lesson. It is far more difficult to describe precisely the changes in facial behavior that reveals understanding and to impart such perceptiveness to less skillful teachers. One way to discover causality is through descriptions of teachers' extraordinary learning and accomplishments and contrasting their behavior with that of others. In modern times, psychologists observed that a Dutch champion chess player spent a huge number of hours playing and studying the game. Researchers later found that nearly all world-class chess players invested much of their lives just as diligently. Subsequent study of world-class men and women in such fields as science, politics, art, music, and writing showed that to the exclusion of much else in their lives, they devoted on average roughly 70 hours a week for a decade to their fields, and that extremely few—perhaps Lincoln and Leonardo da Vinci—excelled nearly all others in more than one rigorous endeavor.

Causality may also be suggested by statistical correlations, that is, the consistent linking of measures in the cases of many individuals. Medical investigators observed, for example, that smokers more often died of lung cancer than did non-smokers. Better causal inferences can be drawn from "statistically-controlled" studies, which take into account other plausible causes. It might be thought, for example, that the pollution and stress of urban life cause people both to smoke and to have cancer. Studies that linked smoking and lung cancer in both cities and rural areas helped to discount that plausible alternate hypothesis.

The "gold currency" of agriculture, medicine, and more recently the social sciences and education is the "randomized experiment" in which the individuals studied are divided into experimental and control groups by lottery. Thus, studies that contrasted animals randomly selected for bouts of exposure to smoke with animals unexposed added much to the creditability of the observable and correlative evidence.

Today, regulations require new drugs and medical treatments to undergo expensive and difficult randomized experiments, usually first on animals and then on human patients. Similarly, social programs are being evaluated in randomized field trials to determine whether they work effectively or not. Economists, policy analysts, and education evaluators began employing randomized experiments in schools in the last several decades, and the results of these are given extra weight in this book.

A single study of any kind can go wrong in many ways. To overcome this limitation this book draws on a number of investigators who have statistically synthesized many studies. A new education method showing superior results in 90% of the studies concerning it has more credibility than a method that shows results in only 60% of the cases. Research synthesis of many studies can also test the possibility that the new method works with a variety of students and circumstances. A robust method shown to work well at many grade levels with boys and girls in cities and suburbs is more desirable than one that only works well in special cases.

Subsequent chapters weigh these considerations. Obviously policymakers and educators must also consider the costs and difficulties of implementing new policies and practices. Some innovations, however, are not only more effective but less costly. Teachers well prepared in their subject matter are usually a better investment than small classes, and, despite conventional beliefs, the Internet and other distance instruction delivery can be both more effective and cheaper than traditional classroom teaching. Thus, both old and new methods should be viewed in terms of efficacy, frugality, ethics, and other considerations.

OVERVIEW AND CAVEATS

The remaining chapters begin with the most fundamental, well-established principles of academic learning within and outside schools. Because children spend approximately 92% of the total hours in the first 18 years of life outside school and under the responsibility of parents, I first describe features of home conditions and parents' behaviors that foster learning before and during the school years. In successive chapters, the book describes the most effective classroom practices and school, district, and state policies. The experimental research on classroom teaching methods is generally far more rigorous than the largely correlative studies carried out at other levels of the education system, and the relative rigor of the research is mentioned where especially relevant.

For several reasons, this book largely concerns research findings of studies that have employed standardized, objective tests of achievement. Federal and state governments require school districts and schools to regularly administer these tests, report their results to parents and the public, and evaluate the progress of schools on the basis of the results. Repeated failure to make achievement progress may force schools to close. After the school years, moreover, such tests are usually the major criterion for entrance into selective colleges, graduate programs, and professional schools. Licensing of many occupations and professions such as law and medicine require such standardized tests. None of this is to argue, of course, that students should avoid writing essays and term papers, conducting science experiments, painting and singing, and carrying out other performance activities in regular classroom work that requires more frequent, informal, and subjective evaluation.

DESIGNED CONCISION AND REPETITION

No single work, to my knowledge, has simultaneously considered effects at all major educational levels of the school system. Despite its broad scope, this book was intended to be concise to facilitate quick assimilation by the very busy people whose responsibility it is for schooling at several levels that the chapters address, namely, the home, classroom, school, district, and state. Because several research findings are available at more than one level, several recommendations, such as increased learning time, are discussed in more than one chapter and chapter section.

It may be important for parents and educators to be reminded of well-established principles as well as to learn about newer findings about their own responsibilities. Equally important, they might also benefit from knowing what works at the school, district, or state level. Parents and policymakers, for example, may play their own roles more effectively and serve as better consumers if they have some understanding about what works at all levels of the system. For these reasons, brief descriptions and explanations are given of effective policies and practices, and in some cases bulleted lists of important details are given.

This book was designed to be concise for an additional reason. The education literature of the last few decades is voluminous. Thousands of articles and books are available. Much of the material is anecdotal and cites little systematic evidence on the causes of learning. As described above, this book employs two filters to select from this huge amount of material—the relative rigor of the research on the policy or practice in question, and the consistency and size of its effect on academic learning. Many references, however, are made to research syntheses, which describe the underlying studies as well as provide detailed descriptions and case studies of how states, districts, and schools successfully implemented proven or promising policies and practices. Readers are referred to these for details about the research and how the policies and practices have been put in place. Conveniently, much of the cited material is available online.

The individual chapters reiterate some themes for several reasons. Research has shown that some effective practices are found in several subjects and at several levels including classrooms and schools, and such confirmatory findings are worth repeating at these levels. For example, both classrooms and schools that employ frequent assessments of student progress tend to achieve more. Also, some readers, such as school board members or state legislators, may focus chiefly on only one level at any one time, and they should have a complete account of the findings at that level. A third reason for repeating several points is that the chapters are somewhat self-contained and can be understood if read separately or in an order other than the sequence in the book.

ACTION RECOMMENDATIONS

Where appropriate, the text offers more detailed and bulleted actions on how the recommendations can be carried out. The recommendations can serve as an index of evidenced-based steps that can be taken at various levels to improve student achievement.

These action recommendations are, of course, supported and explained in the text with the research referenced, but they can be selected to form a discussion outline about what might be most the most effective and suitable improvement steps in a given circumstance. They may also be taken as the state-of-the-art practices to assess existing practices.

CHAPTER 2

ELEMENTS OF STUDENT LEARNING

Knowing how students learn and understanding their motivations to do so help educators teach them. Research studies show the importance of students' capacity to access what they previously learned and the teacher's ability to capitalize on students' interests. An understanding of this research can help educators maximize students' opportunities to retrieve knowledge and acquire new learning.

Multitudes of books and journals are devoted to learning. In this chapter, the vast literature is pared down to several essential factors with the most immediate, direct, and important causal bearings on academic learning. Syntheses of 2,575 study comparisons showed that these factors—students' readiness to learn, the instruction they receive, and the educational environment—are consistently linked with learning (Walberg, 2004, 2006). The rest of this chapter briefly explains the factors and how they affect learning. Subsequent chapters provide greater specificity and describe how homes, classrooms, schools, districts, and states can serve to broaden and deepen their application.

Improving Student Learning: Action Principles for Families, Classrooms, Schools, Districts, and States, pages 9–23

SUBJECT MATTER

Build on Students' Prior Knowledge

Students' present knowledge has the greatest effect on new learning. Syntheses of many studies (see Chapter 3 and also Marzano, 2000, pp. 69–70) show that previous knowledge generates one of the largest known learning effects. Students with a strong knowledge base tend to learn the most. Some knowledge, however, can also stand in the way of new learning (Vosniadou, 2001). Students must learn how to solve internal inconsistencies and revise their ideas when necessary. Students, even older ones, may come to school with beliefs and incomplete understandings that conflict with current explanations of scientific or historical phenomena. An educator's purpose may or may not be to disabuse students of their prior views but often to show them several ways of understanding the same facts, each of which may be appropriate in a given context. As a consequence, students may also acquire tolerance of ambiguity and the views of others. Interest may in fact be enhanced by the presentation of alternative beliefs and explanations.

Two major factors constrain the amount of knowledge and skill that may be acquired and subsequently applied to acquisition of new learning. The first is that only a limited number of items of information can be held in short-term memory. Second, the time required to store an item in long-term memory is 5 to 10 seconds. In chess, mathematics, science, writing, and other fields that have been studied, experts differ from novices in two primary respects: Experts have more information in long-term memory, and they can process new and old information more efficiently.

According to Herbert Simon (1981), the Nobel-prize winning economist and psychologist, the key challenge in information acquisition is allocating our very limited processing capacity to notice, store, and index information. The challenges in using information are retrieving, combining, and applying it. Experts and other high performers tend to elaborately link information items with one another through their indexing systems. Such linking–indexing processes confer the ability to recover information by several pathways. Problem-solving capacity increases with the development of these processes.

The expert's other advantage over novices is "chunking," or the representation of related items of verbal, numerical, spatial, and other items of information as a single condensed symbol. A minute of study, for example, may enable amateur chess players to remember the positions of only a few pieces, but masters may essentially take in a whole board in a few seconds by readily perceiving variations of a few standard chunked patterns of individual pieces. Knowledge and practice enlarge the size of chunks of information assimilated. As individuals practice, chunking enables them to better decide what information to acquire and how to code it efficiently. Self-directed experience and guided practice (or instruction) enables learners to assimilate increasingly larger parts of the information.

Coordinate Subject Matter Across Grade Levels

Students' prior knowledge profoundly affects how quickly and how well they learn new content. Accordingly, America's emphasis over the last decade on K–12 grade-level standards has been intended to avoid unnecessary repetition of the same content in multiple grades while ensuring that students mastered the prerequisite content they need before undertaking new content. With the notable exceptions of Australia, Canada, Germany, and the United States, countries throughout the world have national curricula to avoid these problems. When Japanese students move from one city to another, their new teachers know what they have been taught. Since about 2001, states have been adopting statewide, grade-level standards, and policymakers are discussing national standards—a challenge to the American tradition of state and local control.

Several important books recommend specific content at each grade level of the major school subjects. The modern, best selling advocate of such "core knowledge" is E. D. Hirsch. He began with *Cultural Literacy: What Every American Needs to Know* (1987) which provided a 63-page appendix listing terms and phrases alphabetically. He argued that mastery of these terms and phrases is necessary for participation in American society, and they should, therefore, be taught in school. Hirsch edited or co-edited other books on this theme including, *The Schools We Need and Why We Don't Have Them* (1996) and the Core Knowledge series, which specifies content for each grade level (for example, Hirsch, 1998). These are highly influential works that accelerated the interest in specific subject matter standards and their sequencing across the grades.

In addition to Hirsch's work, organizations of national standing within the United States set forth subject matter standards in mathematics, science, history, social studies, language arts, foreign languages, health, technology, and other subjects. From 28 of these sets of grade-level standards, Marzano (2004) assembled 7,923 terms classified by grade ranges that can serve as candidates for essential ideas for students to learn. In early mathematics, for example, students should learn the meaning of "addition" and "number line;" in high school English they should learn "acronym" and "lyric poem." Marzano makes a detailed case for the importance of such background knowledge for learning. He points out that middle-class students may have more background knowledge learned incidentally outside school, but that students in poverty may need specific instruction in such background knowledge. Thus, Hirsch, Marzano, and others have made a strong case for coordinating content across the grades.

Motivate Students

Just as important as prior knowledge and coordinating subject matter across grades is a student's motivation to learn. Monique Boekaerts' (2002) research synthesis for the United Nations' Educational Practices Series offers insights into students' motivation to learn. Motivational beliefs refer to the opinions, judgments, and values that students hold about objects, events, and various subjects. One student, for example, may find chemistry fascinating, while another may find it irrelevant and boring. Motivational beliefs also stem from the student's opinion of the efficiency or effectiveness of teaching methods. One student may find it tedious to work in groups, while another student may feel that working in a group helps independent productivity. Students' motivation may also be influenced by beliefs about their own self-efficacy, that is, about their own ability and prospects for success in a subject, such as trigonometry or literary criticism.

Research indicates that motivational beliefs often result from learning experiences, such as success or difficulty in solving mathematics problems or positive or negative feedback from writing an essay. Motivational beliefs, therefore, tend to guide students' thinking, feelings, and actions in a subject, and may be optimistic or pessimistic. Once formed, motivational beliefs may be difficult to change.

Students who learn to value acquiring new skills and knowledge may be less dependent on external encouragement to sustain motivation. When students possess an intrinsic motivation to pursue an activity or learn a specific subject, the need for external rewards may be minimal. Students who demonstrate intrinsic motivation report they find gratification in the activity itself.

Many students may appreciate external rewards (e.g., high marks, praise, and compensation) while for other students, ability grouping, competition for grades, and external rewards can diminish their efforts, reinforcing the idea that success is based on innate ability. Students decide how much effort they will allocate to a learning task on the basis of their self-concept of ability and their beliefs about effort. Students may complete tasks they do not value in order to comply with instructions or to receive the reward associated with compliance, but there are better motivators, which are discussed in Chapter 4.

Young children tend to over- and under-estimate their own performance, based on a naïve theory of effort. They may believe that if they want something badly enough and do their best to accomplish it, they will be valued for their effort, which motivates them to keep practicing with high expectations even after repeated failure. By middle childhood, however, some children have lost their belief that their efforts lead to success, especially when their efforts have continually demonstrated result-oriented failure. Such a loss can impede learning because students let their pessimism about past experience and increasingly stronger beliefs about their supposed lack of ability in a particular skill or subject deter them from focusing on the learning activity and trying again. Even though children's understanding of causality changes with age, children resist changing their beliefs about the cause of their own successes and failures in a particular subject area or task. Students who state that they will never succeed at a particular task or subject indicate that they no longer perceive a causal link between their actions and a positive outcome.

Such pessimism can be overcome. By creating learning situations in which students experience success, positive motivation builds up domain-specific positive beliefs as students' knowledge and skills develop. Age- and skill-appropriate tasks require students to predict the effort needed to complete tasks and, once finished, think about how they completed it. This process helps students develop the capacity to self-regulate their own learning more effectively. When students understand how their actions and thinking resulted in a correct solution, strong performance, or positive result, they are more inclined to repeat their behavior and seek to improve upon it. Ironically, students with negative motivational beliefs may be uninterested in process-oriented feedback. They may only want to know whether their answer is correct. Teaching students goal setting techniques and encouraging perseverance are two ways to help them overcome motivational blocks. These topics are further discussed in Chapters 3 and 4.

Employ Incentives

In the world of work, youths and adults are paid to do what others want done; they may intrinsically enjoy their work, but they expect payment for performance. Such thinking is entering or re-entering education. Policymakers' and educators' interest in incentives is rising. Both economists and behavioral psychologists have long assumed that appropriate incentives, both symbolic and real, powerfully shape behavior. If a person seems unresponsive or indifferent to an incentive offered, the observer may not realize the person's perceptions of the incentive's benefits. The incentives may be too small, inappropriate, or too far in the future; the expenditure of time and effort may be too costly.

Nevertheless, Cameron and Pierce (1994) synthesized 96 experimental psychological studies that measured the effects of incentives or rewards on sustained intrinsic motivation to learn and found nearly all positive effects. Similarly, economists have found positive achievement effects of monetary rewards (Kremer, Miguel, & Thornton, 2007). In education, one of the most convincing demonstrations of incentive effects is the Dallas O'Donnell Foundation Advanced Placement Incentive Program. The foundation paid both teachers and students $100 for each Advanced Placement (AP) examination passed—tough examinations potentially offering college credit. For the nine participating Dallas inner-city public schools, the year before the program, 1989, 41 students passed AP exams. Five years later with support of the incentive program, 521 students passed AP exams—a twelve-fold increase.

Advanced Placement incentive programs in the core subjects subsequently spread to seven other Texas school districts, and the passing rate for minority students in the Dallas Independent School District rose to 11 times greater than the U.S. average (Hudgins, 2003). In 2002, 10 Dallas schools had 52 passing AP scores for each 1,000 African American and Hispanic juniors and seniors, compared with 11 for each 1,000 in Texas statewide and 5 for each 1,000 nationwide (Hudgins, 2003). This striking example of the extraordinary effects that can be achieved with external incentives sharply contradicts the prevalent idea in education that all learning must be intrinsically motivated.

INSTRUCTION

Increase Learning Time

American students have the shortest school year among countries of the industrialized world—approximately 180 days in contrast with 190 to 220 days in Western Europe and up to 260 days in Asian countries. American students also do far less homework than students in other economically advanced countries. The American deficit in learning time is undoubtedly a major cause of the American learning gap. Larson's (2001) analysis of 45 studies of how youth spend time documents this deficit:

> U.S. teens spend approximately three-fifths the amount of time on schoolwork that East Asian teens do and four-fifths the time that European teens do. These differences are mostly attributable to American teens doing less homework, estimated at 20 to 40 minutes per day, as compared with 2.0 to 4.0 hours in East Asia and 1.0 to 2.5 hours in Europe.

Efficient use of time during school presents additional challenges. It is wasteful to teach what students already know or what they are as yet incapable of learning. Improving the quality of instruction, then, may be considered an efficient enhancement of learning time.

TABLE 1.   Time Influences on Learning in Various Types of Studies

Area Researched	Relative Effect
Time on task	1.10
Matching time spent to time needed	1.10
Studies of how school time was used	0.49
All estimates	0.47
Efficient time use	0.42
Learning extended by homework and study	0.41
Studies in which instructional time was extended	0.40
Attendance rate	0.32
Earlier start in school or extra preschool	0.27

Wayne Frederick (1993) carried out a comprehensive review of research studies on the influence of time on academic learning for the U.S. Department of Education, which Walberg and Lai (1999) summarized. Table 1 shows various aspects of learning time obtained from Frederick's (1993) review and the estimated influence on achievement. Of 376 estimates of various time effects on learning, 88% showed positive correlations between time and learning. Many of the correlative studies were statistically controlled for student ability or pretests. Given the consistency of the results and their accord with common sense, the implications should be taken seriously, particularly in the light of American students' comparatively limited time in school and in outside study.

The time effects or influences show one of the highest degrees of consistency in educational research. The correlative studies carried out in ordinary uncontrived classrooms have more external validity in that they work well in normal settings. The experimental and quasi-experimental studies have more causal or internal validity, which affords greater confidence that time actually affects achievement. Thus, both correlative and experimental studies tend to show consistent effects. High quality use of instructional time is likely to have a positive effect in even short periods of time, but large amounts of poor teaching or unengaged study may not make much difference. Thus, both quality and quantity of instructional time are necessary for substantial learning.

Space Learning Episodes Over Time

In addition to increasing the amount of productive time spent on academic tasks, revisiting the same academic content over time also increases achievement. In 2007, the U.S. Department of Education issued a practice guide (Pashler et al., 2007) summarizing the most effective instructional methods—methods based on the most rigorous, empirical evidence. One of the leading recommendations is to space learning in episodes over time and arrange the review of key ideas of what is learned after a delay of several weeks to several months.

Based on hundreds of classroom and laboratory experiments on "massed versus distributed practice," the guide concluded that "students typically remember much more when they have been exposed to information on two occasions, rather than one, and when the interval between these two occasions is not less than about 5% of the interval during which the information has to be retained" (Pashler et al., 2007, p. 5). Delayed re-exposure of course material can be achieved through homework assignments, in-class reviews, quizzes, or other instructional exercises. Important curriculum content should be reviewed at least after several weeks, and ideally several months, after first introduction to the content.

Monitor and Encourage Homework Completion

Over two thirds of all 9-year-olds and three quarters of all 13- and 17-year-olds reported doing some homework every day, according to the 1994 Nation's Report Card (Campbell, Reese, O'Sullivan, & Dossey, 1996). As students get older, a greater percentage of them report spending more than 1 hour per day on homework: 39% of 17-year-olds, 37% of 13-year-olds, and 16% of 9-year-olds report spending more than an hour on homework per day. Still, American students spend far less time in school and in out-of-school study than high-achieving Asian students.

An earlier research synthesis (Cooper, 1989) reviewed nearly 120 empirical studies of homework's effects and the ingredients of successful homework assignments. The study revealed that homework completion tended to have significant, positive effects. The average high school student in a class doing homework outperformed 69% of the students in a no-homework class. Cooper's (2006) more recent synthesis of research also indicates consistently positive effects of homework on student achievement.

In addition to enhancing achievement, homework has other potential advantages, including preparing students for independent learning, engaging families in constructive tasks, informing parents of the content of school-based instruction, providing a constructive alternative to television viewing, and enabling the child to practice material without school-based distractions. A well-lit, quiet study area can help avoid distractions that may impede students' completion of homework assignments. Parents can further foster the completion of homework by being aware of homework assignments and establishing and maintaining a scheduled study time for their children. Indeed, regular household schedules for meals, sleep, and so forth in the home reinforce expectations for doing homework (Redding, 2000).

Make Use of Summer School

Summer school can extend school time and raise achievement. Harris Cooper (2006) reviewed 93 summer school evaluations and found significant effects on students' knowledge and skills. Both remedial programs to help lagging students catch up and accelerated programs to allow stronger students to learn more quickly had positive effects.

Encourage Self Instruction

Arguably, successful teachers make themselves unnecessary since students should continue learning after the end of the school day and after they finish their schooling. Students are likely to need to acquire new knowledge and skills for the rest of their lives. Experts' extensive and intensive studies in a variety of fields show that almost universally they have continued to concentrate on their techniques and short-term gains as much as long-term outcomes. Similarly, highly successful students set not only long-term goals but very specific operational goals that can be measured or observed. They devise the best ways to obtain quick, accurate, and informative feedback on their accomplishments of the short-term operational steps. They also assess whether or not the short-term steps are actually leading to the long-term goals.

At one extreme of achievement, an example of world-class chess experts illustrates how the most skilled learners use such principles to teach themselves. Differing from casual players and even those who have played many games for many years, the experts carefully study champion games of previous world masters to understand how their steps and sequences of steps eventually led to checkmate. The highest levels of skill in sports, arts, professions, and other occupations are brought about not only by long hours of practice, but by what the leading scholar on expertise, Anders Ericsson (2007), calls "deliberate practice." This necessary component of outstanding success requires personally setting specific short-term goals, designing methods for attaining immediate feedback on success or failure, and practicing the necessary correctives. Similarly, teachers can employ such principles with their students so students can acquire not only the specific knowledge and skills but disciplined study habits that benefit them throughout their lives.

Foster Academically Constructive Out-of-School Activities

As pointed out below, limiting television exposure appears to be one of the key factors affecting academic achievement, and parents can do much to make children's out-of-school time complement and enhance their formal instruction. As suggested above, children appear to do better in school when parents provide predictable boundaries for their lives, encourage productive use of time, and provide learning experiences as a regular part of family life (Redding, 2000). In families run by calendars, schedules, grocery lists, "to do" lists, shared household chores, reading, studying, and playing mentally challenging games, children may more easily adapt to the responsibilities of school. The disadvantages of poverty may be mitigated by such conditions for learning.

One study (cited in Redding, 2000) found that high-achieving students spend about 20 hours each week outside of school in constructive learning activities, particularly with the support and guidance of parents or other close adults. Music practice, reading, writing, visiting museums, and participation in youth groups engage children in varied learning experiences, keeping them engaged. Parents' support for exploring and working together with their children on hobbies and games multiplies the school's efforts to effectively nurture a child's talents and interests.

Children appear to benefit when their parents know their whereabouts, know their friends, monitor their television viewing, and maintain contact with their teachers. Taking a regular inventory of a child's weekly schedule provides valuable information to parents on how time is being allocated to activities that are in a child's long-term interests. Recreational and social activities, of course, should become a regular part of a child's life, while maintaining the importance of reading and studying.

Deliver High-Quality Instruction

Since Chapter 4 is devoted to teaching practices, only a few general points about instruction that have the most important bearings on students are described in this section to help set the stage. To foster student engagement in learning, teachers can structure learning to build on the student's natural desire to explore and master new skills and knowledge (Vosniadou, 2001). Hands-on activities, such as experiments, observations, and projects, stimulate thinking and challenge students to work independently or actively in groups. Well-facilitated classroom discussions and visits to museums and technology centers in support of students' learning goals provide engaging opportunities to learn. Classroom time should include a variety of activities and minimize passive learning, while encouraging students to take responsibility for their own learning. Teachers can help promote such responsibility and better learning by:

- teaching students how to ask deep, probing questioning of learning materials;
- modeling their own methods of addressing and learning new material;
- teaching problem solving, critical thinking, and comprehension strategies;
- teaching students to plan and monitor their learning, how to set their own learning goals, and how to correct errors;
- helping students learn to allocate study time efficiently;
- using examples and graphics in combination with verbal explanations;
- having students develop their own explanations of materials; and
- creating stimulating activities and tasks that might be practiced outside the classroom.

Chapter 4 is a more extensive exposition of methods of instruction, including special instruction in reading and literacy, mathematics, science, and additional languages.

CLASSROOM, PEER, AND HOME ENVIRONMENTS

Foster Positive Classroom and Peer Group Morale

Researchers measure classroom morale by obtaining student ratings of their perceptions of the classroom group. High, positive morale means that the class members like one another, have a clear idea of the classroom goals, and the lessons are matched to their abilities and interests. Good classroom morale fosters student concentration on academic learning rather than on such distractions as cliques and favoritism. Peer groups outside school and stimulating home environments can provide positive reinforcement of academic achievement by expanding learning time and enhancing its efficiency. Students can learn in both of these environments—among peers and at home—as a reinforcement and enhancement of formal schooling.

Much of classroom learning is a social activity, and participation in the social life of the school may be necessary for learning to occur (Vosniadou,

2001). Children often learn by adopting the activities, habits, vocabulary, and ideas of people in their classrooms. Classroom collaboration in learning can enhance student achievement when focused on academic learning. Social interaction in the classroom can keep students engaged and motivated in academic work. Students may become more productive and improve the quality of their work (in essays, projects, artwork, etc.) when they know that it will be shared with other students.

Encourage Beneficial Outside-School Peer Groups

Educators exert little control over peer groups within and outside school, and the effects of peer groups on learning, though plausible, remain to be rigorously demonstrated. A survey of published experts shows they believe out-of-school peer groups can positively affect learning (Wang, Haertel, & Walberg, 1993). The survey also shows moderate associations between peer group characteristics and learning in a number of statistically controlled studies. A more recent review of 35 outside-school peer group studies (Lauer, Akiba, Wilkerson, Apthorp, Snow, & Martin-Glenn, 2006) showed small positive influences on reading and mathematics performance. However, their own large-scale research showed no such effects, and Scott-Little, Hamann, and Jurs (2002) drew attention to the flaws of many of the studies on this topic. Thus, the empirical research is not definitively consistent, though the idea of constructive peer groups is plausible and has some expert endorsement.

Time spent on traditional extracurricular activities and social clubs seems unlikely to yield substantial achievement effects. But well-designed, well-executed, out-of-school programs featuring achievement may be worthwhile for promoting academic learning. Because the results thus far seem small at best and because educators may have little control over out-of-school time, only further exploration and evaluation of such programs is scientifically justified.

Minimize Time with Mass Media

The last factor affecting learning—mass media, particularly television—can displace homework, leisure reading, and other learning and academically stimulating activities. Television viewing may dull the student's motivation for academic work. Even so, researchers have estimated that high school students spend an average of 20–30 hours a week watching television in contrast to a mere 4 or 5 hours spent on homework weekly. More recently, video games have risen in popularity, also displacing homework time and leisure reading, distracting students from more constructive activity.

Studies of K–12 students indicate that those who watch 4 hours or more of television per day have lower academic achievement than do students who limit their television viewing (Barton & Coley, 2007). Eighth graders who watched more than 5 hours of television per day showed the lowest average mathematics scores in a large international survey. According to a 2004 Child Trends report (as cited in Barton & Coley, 2007), about one third of eighth graders watched 4 hours or more of television on weekdays. Only 19% of children whose parents attended graduate school watched 4 hours or more of television per day, compared to 42% of students whose parents had less than a high school education.

The implications of research on television and video game effects are uncertain because randomized experiments have not been conducted, and it has been difficult to statistically control for rival causes, such as parent education. Moreover, it can easily be envisioned that students may benefit from watching academically constructive programs and discussing them with their parents, classmates, and teachers. For these reasons, educators might best counsel parents to monitor the number and quality of programs their children watch and to limit the amount of time they spend on academically nonproductive programs and video games.

Communicate with Parents

Children throughout the world learn their native language readily and seemingly without effort, while adults beginning a second language find it extraordinarily difficult and frustrating. Thus, nearly universal experience shows that early and sustained immersion in a language has powerful effects. Since language is largely the medium of schooling, its early mastery and sustained encouragement is a key to school success. In language exposure and encouragement, what are the potential effects of parents and educators? As mentioned earlier, of all the hours in the first 18 years of life, American children spend only 8% of their time in school. The other 92% of the hours are the responsibility of their parents, and parents vary widely in their child-rearing practices and in the circumstances they provide for their children.

Hart and Risley's (1995) study showed professional parents, in contrast with low-income parents, not only spoke with their young children much more frequently, but also encouraged them six times more often with positive verbal feedback for good behavior. These parental practices seem to have highly consequential effects on their children's school preparation and success.

Though the causal evidence is neither as clear-cut nor as scientifically rigorous as we might like, the effects of child rearing on children's character and learning seem plausible and are widely believed. For this reason educators may help children by reaching out to their parents and informing them of practices that appear to help children at home and in nonschool hours including afternoons, evenings, and summers.

Because parents are their children's first and perhaps most important teachers, educators might well inform them of their children's progress in school and share ideas about specific practices that can help them at home such as providing a quiet place for reading and homework and discouraging them from watching junk television. Chapter 3 describes home environments and parenting practices that appear conducive to children's learning within and outside school.

CAUSAL PERSPECTIVE

Psychologists and sociologists often study the correlations or coincidence between student socioeconomic status, parent behavior, and achievement, but even substantial and consistent correlations are weak indicators of causality. Affluent, knowledgeable, caring parents, for example, may get their children into special school programs, but it may be these very parental characteristics, rather than the programs, that benefit their children's achievement. Much of the research on environments referred to in the later part of this chapter lacks experimental or sufficient statistical controls to rule out such possibilities. For this reason, the conclusions with respect to classroom morale, peer groups, mass media, and home environments are often tentatively stated, as indicated by such language as "it appears," and the recommendations are offered for exploration and evaluation. Still, people in the real world must often act in uncertainty, and the recommendations are plausible, would seem not to be harmful, and may be efficacious.

Rigorous, randomized, control-group research may eventually settle the questions concerning intervention programs' efficacy to change parent behavior and their effect on children's academic achievement. In the meantime, though not demonstrated, the effects cited are plausible. No one, moreover, showed any harm caused by the programs, and they do give poor children opportunities that come closer to those of middle class children. Even if the effects are minimal, the social capital or constructive relations generated by such programs among parents, educators, children, and others may be valuable in their own right.

In any case, it seems clear that school achievement is positively associated with socioeconomic status and much more closely associated with academically constructive parent behaviors, which influence the students' exposure to mass media and peer groups. Studies of parent programs overall suggest at least a small effect, and eminent scholars support this conclusion and point out specific ways to make the programs more effective.

The learning elements discussed throughout this chapter offer a framework for improving achievement. When teachers build upon students' prior knowledge and stimulate their motivation, students can clearly benefit. Instruction to maximize students' own regulation of academic learning over time can be particularly effective, while increasing the overall amount of time students spend productively engaged in subject matter suitable for them. Teachers' use of quizzes or questions requiring thoughtful answers are among the methods with positive effects. Parents can play a critical motivating and regulating role in coaching children to use their time on fulfilling and productive pursuits that enhance learning. For these reasons, the roles of parents and teachers in student learning are the subjects of Chapters 3 and 4.

CHAPTER 3

FAMILIES

Many factors impinge on academically stimulating qualities of the home environment, which in turn may affect academic readiness and success of students from preschool through college. This chapter examines some of the key features of families and their behavior that appear to limit or improve chances for student success.

FAMILY STRUCTURE

A recent report summarizes data on the demographic factors among American families that appear to affect children's educational outcomes (Barton & Coley, 2007). According to this report, children from single-parent families have a greater risk of poor academic achievement, more behavioral and psychological problems (including substance abuse), and an increased rate of having children outside of marriage. All of these may also negatively affect academic potential.

In 2004, a Kids Count report determined that 31% of children lived in single-parent families in the United States, but rates of single-parent homes differ according to ethnic and racial groups. Based on U.S. Census data, the

Improving Student Learning: Action Principles for Families, Classrooms, Schools, Districts, and States, pages 25–34

Kids Count report indicated that only 35% of African American children lived in two-parent homes.

Poverty is another critical risk factor for poorer academic and life outcomes among children. According to Barton and Coley (2007), "The United States has the greatest inequality in the distribution of income of any developed nation—an inequality that has been rising decade by decade" (p. 14). According to 2005 U.S. Census data for the nation, the top income households had more than 14 times more income than bottom-income households.

PARENTAL BEHAVIORS AND PRIOR LEARNING

Even more powerfully than demographic factors, parental behaviors appear to influence children. Demography, nonetheless, sets the stage and affects both parental behaviors and children's development, particularly their learning prior to entry into school, and especially in those key aspects of language acquisition that are prerequisites for learning to read. In turn, shortcomings in reading ability translate to lower academic achievement.

Children from lower-income families receive significantly reduced exposure to rich vocabulary and less positive verbal affirmation from family members. Mentioned earlier, Hart and Risley (1995) conducted intensive, observational, in-home research on language acquisition in the early life of children (birth to age 4). They estimated that by the end of 4 years, the average child in a professional family hears about 45 million words—nearly double the number of words that children in working-class families hear (25 million) and more than 4 times the number of words, about 10 million, spoken to children in low-income families.

Though vocabulary differences between the groups were small at 12 to 14 months of age, by age 3 sharp differences emerged, which correlated with parents' socioeconomic status (SES). Children from families receiving welfare had vocabularies of about 500 words; children from middle/lower SES families about 700; and children from families in higher socioeconomic brackets had vocabularies of about 1,100 words, more than twice that of children from families receiving welfare. Parents of higher SES, moreover, used "more different words, more multi-clause sentences, more past and future verb tenses, more declaratives, and more questions of all kinds" (Hart & Risley, 1995, pp. 123–24). Entwisle and Alexander (1993) also found that differences in children's exposure to vocabulary and elaborate use of language multiply further at ages 5 and 6, when children enter school.

Children in poorer families are also less likely to have parents regularly read to them than children in wealthier families (Barton & Coley, 2007). Sixty-two percent of parents of 3-to-5-year-old children from the highest income quintile read to their children every day. In the lowest income quintile, only 36% of parents read to their 3-to-5-year-old child. Children in two-parent families were more likely to have someone read to them regularly than were children in single-parent homes (63% vs. 53%). Also, mothers with higher educational attainment read to their children more often. Only 41% of mothers with less than a high school diploma read to their child or children regularly, compared with 55% of mothers who are high school graduates, and 72% of mothers with college degrees.

Sticht and James (1984) emphasize that children first develop vocabulary and comprehension skills before they begin school by listening, particularly to their parents. As they gain experience with written language between the 1st and 7th grades, their reading ability gradually rises to the level of their listening ability. Highly skilled listeners in kindergarten make faster reading progress in the later grades, which leads to a growing ability gap between initially skilled and unskilled readers.

This growing gap seen in reading skill levels reflects inequalities by race/ethnicity and SES. Although in the United States there are numerically more low-income Whites than similarly low-income African Americans and Hispanics, minority groups have disproportionately higher rates of poverty. Although policy research has increased in recent decades on these SES issues, far more research has been conducted with African American families than with Latino families. Wigfield and Asher (1984) offer their conclusive findings in the authoritative *Handbook of Reading Research*:

> The problems of race and socioeconomic status (SES) differences in achievement have been at center stage in educational research for nearly three decades. Research has clearly demonstrated that such differences exist; black children experience more difficulty with reading than white children, and the discrepancy increases across the school years. Similarly, children from lower SES homes perform less well than children from middle-class homes, and here too the difference increases over age. (p. 423)

Not only do lower SES families offer fewer linguistic experiences and skills to their children, they also evidence other behaviors that tend to impede children's early preschool development. For example, mothers of low-SES often demonstrate weak problem-solving skills of their own, but nevertheless tend to take over children's experimentation with problem solving, a realization of a lack of confidence in their children's abilities (Wigfield & Asher, 1984). In other studies, low-income parents discouraged their children with negative feedback about 275,000 times, about 2.2 times the amount employed by parents with professional jobs. These parents with greater incomes "gave their children more affirmative feedback and responded to them more often each hour they were together" (Hart & Risley, 1995, pp. 123–24). Parents with professional jobs encouraged their children, by the time they reached age 4, with positive feedback 750,000 times, about 6 times as often as low-income parents did. Such parenting behaviors predicted about 60% of the variation in vocabulary growth and language use of 3-year-olds. Furthermore, low-SES parents tend to "view school as a distant, rather formidable institution over which they have little control" (Wigfield & Asher, 1984, p. 429), an attitude very unlikely to help their children adopt an enthusiastic view of schooling. Behaviorally, too, children of low-income families are "disadvantaged" because these children, upon entry into formal schooling, are often "lacking the habits of conduct" expected, such as working independently and attentively on a given task (Entwisle & Alexander, 1993, p. 405).

These factors stifle prior learning and behavioral readiness for school and result in "Matthew effects" of the academically poor getting poorer and the rich getting richer (Walberg & Tsai, 1984). Ironically, although improved instructional programs may benefit all students, they may confer greater advantages on those who are initially advantaged. For this reason, the first 6 years of life and the "curriculum of the home" may be decisive influences on academic learning. These effects appear pervasive in school learning, including the development of reading comprehension and verbal literacy (Stanovich, 1986).

READING AND ACADEMIC ACHIEVEMENT

Along with some attitudinal and behavioral factors of prior learning in the home, much of this chapter primarily focuses on the children's developing vocabulary and other pre-reading skills, because reading proficiency is the most important goal in the early grades and because learning in most subjects depends on reading skills. The National Assessment of Educational Progress 2007 *Nation's Report Card* for reading shows, however, that only 33% of fourth graders in the United States are at or above proficient in reading (National Center for Education Statistics, 2007). Among eighth graders in American public schools, the percentage of proficient readers is similarly low, 31%, a rate which has not changed since 1992. Millions of children who fall substantially behind in reading in the early grades are unlikely to catch up without intensive intervention.

A lack of proficiency in reading skills leads to underachievement in other subjects and early academic disengagement, which often magnifies over time to the point of dropping out of high school. Conversely, a strong literacy foundation in early childhood leads to high school graduation and post-secondary schooling. At this time, too many children are not getting that foundation. Nearly a million ninth graders will not earn a diploma in 4 years (Education Trust, 2007), which means that about one in four students are not graduating from high school on time. Among African American and Latino students, the high school graduation rate is significantly lower, as one third of them currently do not receive high school diplomas. High school achievement is similarly low. The *Nation's Report Card* (Grigg, Donahue, & Dion, 2007) reports that in 2005, the U.S. 12th grade reading achievement declined for all but the top performers, and less than one quarter (23%) of the U.S. 12th graders perform at or above proficiency in mathematics. Only 35% of the nation's 12th graders performed at or above the proficient reading level in 2005.

PRESCHOOL PROGRAMS

Can developmental and early educational programs diminish growing achievement gaps that begin in early childhood and increase as children enter and proceed through school?[1] An analysis of 48 published articles on early childhood interventions to improve home environments shows positive but small (0.2) overall effects (Bakermans-Kranenburg, van Izendoorn, & Bradley, 2005), with randomized intervention studies showing a smaller average effect size of 0.13. Children of middle class parents benefited more from the programs than those from poor families—the Matthew effect. One reason for limited program effects overall is that the program sessions were usually limited in time and took place over only a small fraction of the child's life. Moreover, parents, particularly those in poverty, may or may not be able to fulfill the program requirements.

Head Start is by far the largest and longest enduring early childhood program. Intended to help children in poverty from birth to age five, it began in 1965 under President Johnson, providing grants to local public and private non-profit and for-profit agencies to establish an array of services, including dental, optical, mental, and physical health services, nutrition, and parental involvement and education. Head Start now serves over 900,000 low-income children and their families each year.

However, a 1985 synthesis of about 300 studies of Head Start and other early childhood programs revealed that their moderate immediate effects on achievement and other cognitive tests faded within 2 to 3 years; that is, program students did better on achievement tests than control-group students at the end of the program, but the difference between the groups diminished to insignificance (White, 1985). Since 1985, the programs attempted to improve by concentrating on children's academic readiness,

---

[1]Since this book concerns Kindergarten through twelfth grade and because preschool research has been difficult to conduct rigorously and the findings are inconsistent and controversial, actionable recommendations are not offered in this section though some tentative implications are discussed.

and reviews since then have been slightly more encouraging (Currie, 2001; Karoly et al., 1998).

A recent large-scale study by the U.S. Department of Health and Human Services (HHS) found that Head Start helps children make gains in cognitive development that narrows the achievement gap. In May 2005, the first year findings from the impact study—a Congressionally mandated study that requires HHS to evaluate the impact of Head Start on the children and families it serves—offered evidentiary support for Head Start. Based on a rigorous, randomized experimental design, the study demonstrated that after less than one school year, Head Start narrowed achievement gaps by 45% in pre-reading skills and by 28% in pre-writing skills and positively impacted vocabulary skills as well. Head Start apparently changed parent behavior, too, including increasing the frequency of parents reading to their children.

Another rigorous, large-scale, random-assignment evaluation of Head Start showed small positive effects on parental behavior and on children through age 3 (Mathematica Policy Research, 2002). The particular Head Start project studied was designed to enhance children's development and health, strengthen family and community partnerships, and to deliver new services to low-income families with pregnant women, infants, or toddlers. The 17 project instances investigated included 3,001 families and showed small, temporary effects.

AN EFFECTIVE PRESCHOOL PROGRAM

So far, this chapter considered learning in the preschool years and parents' contribution to an environment that stimulates learning, either through actions of their own or in collaboration with family–child programs like Head Start. Unlike other early childhood programs that emphasize "developmental appropriateness," self-esteem, and play, one program, the Chicago Child–Parent Centers (CPC), directly teaches academic language and number skills, which concerns one of the teaching factors not yet discussed— the quality, including content, of instruction. This program emphasizes the acquisition of language and pre-mathematical experiences through teacher-directed, whole-class instruction, small-group activities, and field trips for preschoolers, beginning at age 3.

The program also features intensive parental participation in each center's parent resource room. A landmark study of the CPC —the only long-term study of an academically focused early learning program—demonstrated significant long-term effects and cost-effectiveness of this academically oriented family-support program (Reynolds, 2000; Reynolds, Temple, Robertson, & Mann, 2001).

Compared with matched control-group children, the 989 participating CPC children showed higher cognitive skills at the beginning and end of kindergarten, and they maintained greater school achievement through the later grades. Furthermore, by age 20, CPC graduates had substantially lower rates of special education placement and grade retention than the control group, a 29% higher rate of school completion, and a 33% lower rate of juvenile arrest. A cost–benefit analysis showed that, at a per-child program cost of $6,730 for 18 months of part-day services, the age-21 benefits per child totaled $47,759 in increased economic well-being and reduced expenditures for remediation. Few education studies have either followed children as long or calculated the costs and benefits of the programs.

In CPC, program staff coordinate preschool activities with continuing kindergarten services in neighborhood schools. The program involves parents by engaging them in academically stimulating experiences for their children at home, such as teaching them numbers, letters, and colors. The results support productivity factors described in Chapter 2—namely, the home environment; the quality of instruction, particularly its academic emphasis; the amount of instruction, since the children were given the advantage of extra academic time; and contributed to their prior learning before starting school. Both the program and the evaluation are unique.

Most programs lack the CPC features, and a review of evaluations (Karoly et al., 1998) found that about half the early childhood intervention programs showed no significant effect on achievement. As the CPC evaluation and others illustrate, even though most early childhood programs show small and unsustainable effects, a few programs may show substantial effects. The continuing research task is to find the exemplary features of programs that work well, which is easier said than done because such research is likely to require randomization and long-term study.

K-12 SCHOOL-LEVEL PARENT PROGRAMS

In addition to the preschool programs discussed in the preceding section, a variety of programs teach parents how to enhance the home environment in ways that may benefit their children's learning. Parents may be encouraged, for example, to support their children's academic, social, and emotional learning by participating in parent education and home-visit programs beginning in the preschool years (Redding, 2000). The home visit model typically targets parents of preschool age children, some as early as birth, and appears most effective when combined with group meetings with other parents to reinforce a collegial and non-threatening atmosphere of learning.

Conduct Effective School Parenting Programs

As described by Redding (2000), workshops and courses conducted by educators, psychologists, and pediatricians have the advantages of research-based content and access to professional knowledge. The programs can teach parents ways to improve the quality of cognitive stimulation and verbal interactions that produce immediate, positive effects on their child's intellectual development.

Home Visiting: Home visit programs enable focused, personalized coaching in the natural setting of the home, though this feature may be labor-intensive and expensive. Studies of early home visits have showed positive gains and good economic returns; some studies are more rigorous than others. (See Daro testimony and citations: http://www.chapinhall. org/sites/default/files/Daro%20Early%20Support%20for%20Family%20 Act%20testimony_1.pdf). Small-group sessions led by trained parents in homes and schools are less expensive, encourage parents' attachment to the school, and allow them to share experiences and assist one another.

According to Redding, the two most common challenges in parent education are providing staff to organize and provide programs and attracting parents to participate. To meet the challenge of staffing, Redding suggests partnering with health and religious organizations that conduct childhood outreach programs. To attract parents, programs could seek parental suggestions for programming; engage parents in recruitment efforts; and use field-tested, proven models and curricula.

Language Stimulation: Several kinds of parent–child interactions may enhance a child's success in school, including seriously conversing with the child daily, reading with the child and talking about what is read, storytelling, and letter writing (Redding, 2000). As parents increasingly lead busy lives, spending several minutes a day in fully engaged private conversation with a child can make an important difference. Furthermore, verbal interactions can reinforce the affective bonds between parents and children, and affectionate communication affirms the joy of learning. Parents can reinforce their children's attempts to expand vocabulary use, while ridicule about faulty new vocabulary use can cripple children's natural learning and experimentation process. Museums, libraries, zoos, historical sites, and cultural centers provide enriched contexts for conversation and inquiry.

Rigorously Evaluate Parent Programs

Two bodies of research on the parents' role emerged over recent decades to answer questions regarding the impact of parent involvement. One strand of research investigates the effects of parent's naturally occurring involvement, and another body of research evaluates the effects of interventions designed to improve parents' involvement in children's schooling. In a recent review of non-randomized research on parent involvement (Pomerantz, Moorman, & Litwack, 2007), parents' naturally occurring school-based involvement suggests fairly consistent and occasionally substantial positive influences on achievement.

Definitive randomized research based on programs that seek to involve parents in the schools and their children's education is unavailable; however, some longitudinal designs take into account children's achievement progress. These suggest that the value of school-based involvement—regardless of parents' socioeconomic status or educational attainment—is not great. A research synthesis of 41 studies that evaluated K–12 parent involvement programs concluded that there is little empirical support for their efficacy to improve student achievement, and changing parent, teacher, and student behavior (Mattingly, Prislin, McKenzie, Rodriquez, & Kayzar, 2002). The synthesis found few quality (randomized, experimental) studies of parent involvement programs, and most studies lacked the necessary rigor to provide valid evidence of program effectiveness. Thus, it seems possible that the programs may improve outcomes, but the research may be insufficiently rigorous to prove their efficacy. Obviously, both rigorous research and continuing evaluation of local programs is in order.

Communicate with Parents

Despite the lack of definitive research, parents may benefit from greater knowledge of home practices that promote their children's learning before and after the school day. Students may also benefit from communication between their parents and their teachers that flows in both directions. Students appear to show higher levels of achievement when parents and teachers understand each other's expectations and communicate regularly about the child's learning habits, attitudes towards school, social interactions, and academic progress (Henderson & Mapp, 2002).

Schools that provide incentives or recognition for teachers to maintain close connections with parents tend to sustain a quality, disciplined, educational environment. Redding (2000) recommends a variety of communication strategies:

- parent–teacher–student conferences that stimulate positive and constructive feedback on student work (such as through a portfolio) with the structure of a meeting agenda
- report cards (daily, monthly, or quarterly) that include written two-way communication

- newsletters with contributions by parents
- open door parent–teacher conferences at designated times, such as 30 minutes before school each morning
- e-mails to parents or general listserve bulletins

Redding affirms observations made by sociologist James S. Coleman: When the families of children in a school associate with one another, social capital is increased; children are watched over by a larger number of caring adults; and parents discuss standards, norms, and the experiences of child rearing. Children may benefit when the adults around them share basic values about child rearing, often communicate with one another, and give their children consistent support and guidance aligned with thoughtfully defined values.

Thus, eminent authorities and some research suggest that educators can reach out to parents to encourage them to stimulate the development of their children's academic achievement. A variety of programs discussed in this chapter provide insights into the planning and conduct of new programs.

CHAPTER 4

CLASSROOMS

A learning element discussed in Chapter 2 central to classroom learning is the quality of the instructional experience as provided by and managed by teachers. Simply put, research shows that the methods of instruction that teachers employ, as well as the content of the curriculum they teach, are key factors affecting learning in K–12 classrooms. Teachers who provide good instruction also make use of several chief factors that affect learning: prior learning, coordinating content across grade levels, time spent on learning, motivation, and classroom morale.

With these learning factors in mind, this chapter focuses on the teaching of reading (and writing and speaking), second language acquisition, mathematics, and science. Many citizens—legislators, parents, and educators—long believed that these subjects should be given special emphasis in education. The consensus on the importance of these topics prompted the International Bureau of Education, a division of United Nations Educational, Scientific, and Cultural Organization (UNESCO) to ask me to commission and edit a series of booklets on educational practices, addressing them. These booklets, all written by eminent authorities, were distributed worldwide; the recommendations in this chapter derive from several volumes in the series.[1]

____

[1] The recommendations are based upon the Educational Practice Series of booklets for educational leaders that I commissioned as the series editor. The booklets may be consulted

____

Improving Student Learning: Action Principles for Families, Classrooms, Schools, Districts, and States, pages 35–57

    35

GENERAL PRACTICES

Students learn best in a supportive classroom climate that offers coherent content, thoughtful discourse, practice and application activities, strategy teaching, cooperative learning, goal-oriented assessment, and expectations for high achievement.[2] The principles of effective practices presented in this section serve as a guide for developing successful teaching methods, though they require adaptation to local context, subject area, grade level, and type of student population. Each principle can be addressed individually but should be considered in relationship to the other principles of effective teaching.

Build on Prior Learning

Teaching within a "zone of proximal development" means avoiding material students already mastered and that which they are yet incapable of learning. Instead, use explanation, modeling, and coaching until students develop independent proficiency to learn further on their own. According to educational research, assignments should be sufficiently varied and interesting, offer new information that builds on students' prior knowledge, contain a reasonable level of difficulty, and show a high rate of success with proper time and effort. In order for activities to have full impact, teachers need to thoughtfully choose them, present them, monitor the process and results, and conduct follow-up planning for necessary re-teaching in areas of low performance and quality.

Align Curriculum and Instruction with Standards

Effective teachers enable learning by creating coherent networks of knowledge. Most states now have specified standards for acceptable grade-level achievement in many subjects; all have such standards for reading and mathematics. However, as a result of competing demands from textbook publishers, policymakers, and externally driven assessments, curricular content may nevertheless lack coherence, sufficient depth, strong relation-

---

for further information and many references to research and practice. All are available in English on the Bureau's website, http://www.ibe.unesco.org/en/services/publications/educational-practices.html, and many have been translated into several languages. All may be freely downloaded, reproduced, and republished. Full citations and web addresses for each are presented in the references.

[2]Recommendations in this section are derived from J. Brophy's (1999) UNESCO pamphlet, *Teaching.*

ships to student interests and their cultural context, or integration with necessary skill development.

Teachers must thoughtfully incorporate these features to complement the given texts, policies, assessments, and curriculum. The curriculum should have as its primary goal the fostering of understanding, whereby students learn individual elements in a broader network of related content and express the content in their own words, as well as connect it to prior knowledge. When students appreciate and value what they are learning, while understanding and agreeing with the reasons for learning it, they are better able to extend the curriculum of the school to other important contexts.

Allocate Learning Time Wisely

Efficient Classrooms

Providing opportunity to learn is less about the breadth of curriculum coverage than it is about maximizing the use of time. Research indicates that teachers who approach classroom management as a process of establishing an effective learning environment tend to be more successful than teachers who primarily act as disciplinarians. Effective teachers use management techniques that encourage students' cooperation during classroom time, sustain their engagement in learning activities, and offer motivation for independent work.

When teachers show a sense of purposefulness about time, they proceed through lessons smoothly following a timely instructional plan, begin and end lessons on time, keep transitions short, and support their students to get started quickly and maintain focus. Activities and assignments should feature stimulating variety and optimal challenges to help students sustain their engagement and minimize disruptions due to boredom or other distractions.

Successful teachers consistently and clearly articulate their expectations. They teach students strategies and procedures for participating in recurring activities such as whole-class lessons, working in pairs, small-group projects, transitions between activities, handling personal belongings, completing assignments, and knowing how and when to ask for assistance. Teachers' should focus on building students' capacity for managing their own learning, such that teachers have to micromanage instructional tasks less and less as the school year progresses.

Practice and Application

Good teachers devise activities or assignments that provide students with opportunities to practice a skill or apply content. Research indicates that skills practiced to the point of automaticity (without deliberation) tend to be retained indefinitely, whereas skills only partially mastered tend to degenerate over time. When students practice a skill across varied time periods in a variety of tasks, they sustain motivation more effectively. Teachers should provide ample opportunities for review, reflection, and application of knowledge in activities throughout the day. Reflection activities should include opportunities for students to ask follow-up questions, share task-related observations or experiences, compare opinions, or deepen their appreciation of what they have learned by applying it to their home and community life.

Homework

Homework assignments, realistic in length and difficulty, extend learning time. Such assignments should be graded and reviewed in class the following day. Feedback to students should be informative rather than evaluative to help students understand their progress with respect to major goals and to correct errors or misconceptions. More complex tasks and learning sets of knowledge require more practice. Such projects require students to self-regulate their learning to some degree as well as apply conceptual understanding to practical problems and questions.

Provide High-Quality Instruction

Previewing Learning

According to numerous research studies, students accelerate their learning when lessons and activities begin with advance organizers or previews, providing a framework for modeling a skill. Such introductions facilitate students' learning by communicating the purpose and importance of activities, connecting the assignment or topic with prior knowledge, and cueing students to responses required by the lesson. Well-planned lesson orientations also stimulate students' motivation to learn, and students can then set goals for the content and learning activity. Effective teachers may use a range of strategies, including calling attention to the goals of the activity, providing an overview of the main ideas or steps, conducting goal-setting with students, or using pretests to activate students' thinking around the main points and their own questions.

When making presentations, providing explanations, or giving demonstrations, effective teachers project enthusiasm for the content and organize it in order to maximize clarity and coherence. Research recommends:

- presenting new information by referencing students' prior learning;
- proceeding in small, sequenced steps in an easy to follow format;

- using pacing, gestures, and other oral communication skills to support comprehension;
- avoiding vague language and digressions that disrupt continuity;
- eliciting students' responses regularly; and
- finishing with a review of main points, stressing areas for integration and application.

Teachers should also help students follow the flow and structure of the content by using outlines or graphic organizers that depict relationships, study guides that call attention to key ideas, or task organizers that help students keep track of the steps involved as well as the strategies they used to complete the steps.

Engaging Thought

To develop students' capacity to develop and articulate their ideas, effective teachers plan sequences of questions designed to develop systemic and sophisticated understanding of content, build upon prior knowledge, and explore subject-related applications and personal meanings. Some closed-ended questions can be useful to elicit prior knowledge, but open-ended questions will provoke more thought, discussion, and debate. Questions should be posed to the whole class for consideration, with opportunity to engage in discussion in pairs, small groups, and the larger class. Teachers should invite students to develop explanations, make predictions, debate alternative approaches to problems, or otherwise consider creative and useful applications of the content. The teacher's role is to motivate students to clarify or justify their assertions, rather than accepting them indiscriminately.

Modeling Cognitive Skills

Effective teachers model a range of study skills and learning strategies. Cognitive modeling, or "think alouds," demonstrates teachers' thinking process while performing a task. Integrating self-regulation and self-evaluation strategies into think alouds is particularly useful for novice learners. Strategies to be mastered by students include:

- repeating material to remember it more effectively;
- paraphrasing in their own words while using prior knowledge;
- outlining material to highlight its structure;
- keeping track of strategies and the degree of success with them; and
- affect monitoring (that is, awareness of concentration and fear of failure).

Pairing or Grouping Students

Numerous research studies report strong benefits of cooperative, small-group learning among students. In groups of two to four, students strengthen their motivation, task engagement, ability to work with individuals different from themselves, and verbal processing of subject matter. Cooperative learning methods work most effectively when each group member is held accountable for accomplishing the activity's learning goals, develops individual content, or skill mastery can be individually assessed. In order to be most productive in working in small groups, teachers may need to show their students how to listen, share, integrate the ideas of others, and handle disagreements constructively. During small-group work, teachers should circulate to monitor progress and provide needed coaching, correction, and thoughtful observation.

Monitoring Progress

Formal tests, performance evaluations, and informal evaluations of students' work offer a varied perspective on students' knowledge and skills, especially when those evaluations are aligned with curricular goals and instructional methods. Assessment portfolios should ideally include standardized tests, publisher-supplied curriculum tests, teacher-developed tests, and everyday learning activities and participation. Pen and paper tests can be supplemented by performance evaluations of laboratory exercises, artistic performances, reports and oral presentations graded using a rubric or checklist, and essays. Assessments that check progress, in particular, can provide useful information to:

- identify learner needs, misunderstandings, or misconceptions that may require attention;
- suggest potential adjustment in curriculum goals, instructional materials, or teaching plans; and
- detect weaknesses in the assessment activities or process.

Appropriate Expectations

Educational research indicates that teachers' expectations regarding what their students are capable of accomplishing (with support from the teacher) tend to shape students' expectations of themselves. Teachers' expectations should be situated in a realistic and respectful understanding of students' strengths, talents, and areas of difficulty. Establishing a pyramid of achievement levels (such as basic, proficient, and advanced) for students may help them better assess their own level of achievement and set goals for advancing to higher levels. Rather than emphasizing how students compare with their classmates or with nationally normed groups of students, it is more useful to assess students' progress based on previous levels of mastery.

It is better for teachers to encourage students to achieve their best and for students to stretch their range of inquiry, rather than protect them from mild failure or embarrassment.

New Media

Expanded access to electronic media offers today's teachers and students dynamic new ways to teach and learn.[3] In the long run, instructional technology is likely to prove more effective, cost efficient, and time saving than regular classroom teaching. Even now, in the most extensive synthesis of research covering 232 control-group studies, Bernard, Abrami, and Lou (2004) found that student achievement, attitude, and retention were the same for classroom and distance education over the Internet.

Eight separate (meta-analytic) reviews revealed that computer-based instruction had moderate to large positive effects on student achievement (Kulik, 2001). Students gained more knowledge in computer classes and took more pleasure in the instruction than their counterparts in standard classrooms. Gifted students, in particular, derived great benefits from computer-based tutoring and accelerated classes.

Electronic works can add sound, color, animation, and interactivity to text, adding stimulation for engagement. The Internet offers an instantaneous and free (or inexpensive) access to content. When low-speed internet connections, slow computers, or both are a concern, CDs or DVDs provide a large amount of material, which can be easily distributed at a low cost. Providers' websites or files on local servers can also provide access to materials for individual students or staff in education centers, schools, libraries, and classrooms—both for small-scale specific distribution or for uniform, large-scale curriculum adoption. But CDs and DVDs cannot be easily updated like material on the Internet, material which, of course, like printed matter, needs to be vetted for accuracy, currency, and appropriateness of content.

In addition to broadening accessibility and the ability to engage students, computers may also help teachers. For example, computer-based reading programs have the option of including automated evaluation and progress tracking of reading comprehension and can more effectively accommodate different starting points and learning paces. Rapid, ongoing feedback is available through online formats. Strategically adding some graphics and images is generally helpful and worth the additional file space when they are used to substantially aid text comprehension. Also, computers can automatically evaluate the reading difficulty of text, which can be helpful to both individual learners and teachers providing content for a large group. Methods such as Dale-Chall and Flesch-Kincaid examine basic statistics

---

[3]This subsection on the use of new media is mainly derived from Shih and Weekly (2005), *Using New Media.*

about text, such as the average word length, average sentence length, and average paragraph length. Text can then be matched with educational purposes, students' interests, and reading levels.

TEACHING LITERACY SKILLS

Chapters 2 and 3 explained the importance of early childhood learning and made recommendations for the family's role in helping develop a child's vocabulary, grammar, and oral language—all as a foundation for learning to read. Here, recommendations for the formal teaching of reading in school are considered, as well as the teaching of writing and listening (Wallace, Stariha, & Walberg, 2004) which complement and augment reading facility. The following principles of effective reading and writing instruction derive from studies of children and adults. For reading in particular, research emphasizes the importance of mastery of two related processes: word recognition and comprehension. The principles below, when taken together, represent a balanced approach to instruction to maximize both word recognition and comprehension.[4]

Activate Prior Knowledge

As discussed in earlier chapters, the effects of prior knowledge on learning are greater than any other single factor. In reading, a student's level of prior knowledge—knowledge of the world, cultural knowledge, subject-matter knowledge, interpersonal knowledge, and linguistic knowledge—tends to influence interest in a subject and depth of comprehension. Effective reading teachers choose texts carefully, based on design, cultural appropriateness, and grade level. However, because accessing prior knowledge may not be automatic and its connections to the material at hand may not be immediately recognized by students, spending time to activate prior knowledge about a text will increase students' comprehension and interest in the material. Asking students to express what they know about a topic before reading, inviting students to ask questions about what they think they will learn from a text, and asking them what they want to learn more about prepare them to better appreciate each text. Reading should then be followed by conversation, reflection, summarization of key points, and respectful critique.

---

[4]This section is derived from the recommendations in the UNESCO pamphlets *Teaching Reading*, by Pang, Muaka, Bernhardt, & Kamil (2003), and *Teaching Speaking, Listening, and Writing* by Wallace, Stariha, & Walberg (2004).

Relate Learning to Social Background

A person's development of knowledge occurs through experience with their environment, culture, and personal interactions. Having richly textured cultural knowledge affects a reader's understanding and appreciation of written text. In order to appreciate certain kinds of humor, for example, the writer and reader must share an understanding and common base of knowledge. Having more cultural knowledge enriches reading comprehension of a wider variety of written texts. Parents and teachers should choose reading materials that are culturally appropriate and also broaden the child's current sphere of knowledge. When introducing texts, it is useful to explain new culturally situated vocabulary, experiences, and knowledge.

Activate Motivation

Select Engaging Reading Matter

Students benefit from having an array of experiences with reading for different purposes: entertainment, religious reflection or prayer, learning new information, career preparation or enhancement, personal development, or improving reading as a skill. When reading material connects with students' natural motivations, personal goals, and desired purposes for reading, they are more likely to enjoy it and extend time doing it. Exposing students to a range of different types of texts (fiction, textbooks, news articles, magazine articles, and storybooks) as well as genres (news articles and editorials; narrative and lyric poetry; historical, contemporary, and futuristic fiction) help students and teachers to identify reading matter that matches students' natural inclinations and needs. Interacting with the same or similar texts in different ways (writing task, small-group project) maintains interest and develops facility with different types of reading purposes. Students develop independent discipline to read more often when they are encouraged to read materials aligned with their interests, hobbies, and life goals. Teaching appropriate reading strategies that correspond to texts and real-life tasks, such as reading for general meaning, recalling specific information, understanding inferences and implications, skimming, and scanning also develop facility.

Select Engaging Texts of Appropriate Difficulty

Children should have thoughtful guidance from knowledgeable adults in choosing texts appropriate to their reading level. Vocabulary, word length, grammatical complexity, and sentence length generally indicate the difficulty of a text. Teachers can help students assess their own capacity to interpret a text and find it interesting by helping them to learn how to assess a text at a glance by skimming or trying a few sentences or paragraphs to get a feel for the writing style and difficulty. For non-native speakers, texts should be chosen that facilitate understanding and interest, while introducing new concepts, vocabulary, and information.

Increase Learning Time

Teachers should encourage reading by providing numerous opportunities to do so—both inside and outside of class. When children read more often, they strengthen their repertoire of vocabulary and knowledge, as well as reading comprehension, speed, and fluency. Students should have ample access to books and reading materials at home and at school, and sustained silent reading programs can be used to create disciplined and enjoyable reading time. Also, when other children, teachers, or interested adults ask a child questions to invite conversation about what they are reading, it encourages them to verbalize their thoughts and feelings regarding texts.

Connect Reading with Writing

Writing helps strengthen connections between oral and written language. Research indicates the benefits of guiding children through the process of writing down what they have experienced. For young children, learning to write and spell helps develop their understanding of conventions and symbols of printed text. Teachers can help students to develop writing by demonstrating writing down children's words as they talk about experiences (e.g., spring vacation). The children can then read the text and connect what was said to the written form of it.

Writing involves a wide array of tasks and skills that can be overwhelming to beginners. Because students often do not know how much they know about a topic, writing, like reading, requires elicitation of prior knowledge through various "invention" strategies—such as journalistic questioning (who, what, when) or brainstorming (free association)—which help develop ideas about the subject and discover connections to related topics. Out of this prewriting development—which can include outlining and note taking—it is important to identify a central idea, then draft and revise the piece of writing, perhaps more than once, in a recursive process of topic exploration, further drafting, and evaluation. Writing speed may increase with the production of a detailed outline and an initial draft rather than concentrating on the logical, grammatical, and stylistic concerns of the document. Writing on the computer offers a number of advantages when keyboarding skills are developed enough to help.

Recent research on writing instruction suggests that effective writing programs integrate product, process, and genre writing into a coherent whole. The "product approach" to writing involves coaching students on the final result of writing—a logical, error-free essay or document. Teachers provide a model text or sample, which students read, analyze, and then reproduce. The "process approach" to writing guides the writer through stages of invention, drafting, revising, proofreading, and producing the final draft. Teaching "genre writing" involves helping students to identify, compare, and contrast writings in different fields, such as science and literature.

Students may also need practice in writing nonacademic materials such as letters, forms, resumes, and lists. Recommended instructional strategies are to

- teach stages of the writing process;
- provide models of high-quality writing and discuss what makes the samples well-written;
- discuss audience expectations of acceptable writing and how each genre uses different writing styles;
- select writing topics of personal interest to students and reinforce tasks that students will need to master to further develop their writing; and
- teach students real-life writing tasks such as completing forms, letters, and charts.

Develop Speaking Skills

Just as writing can strengthen students' reading skills, learning formal speaking skills can complement writing and reading skills. Students better develop their formal speaking capacity when they receive coaching during each phase of speech preparation and delivery. Teachers help students improve their presentation as early as the planning phase when the overall purpose, sequence, and scope of the speech is determined. Just as with reading and writing, practice with different genres—such as informative, persuasive, comical, satirical—and their respective purposes and styles helps students increase their versatility.

Students benefit from encouragement and guidance to try many different styles of speaking, while also learning to tune in to the listeners' response to each style. Learning how to adapt the speaking rate, volume, precision in pronunciation, and use of dialect to the audience and purpose of their communication will give students greater flexibility and success in building relationships through their speech. Students benefit from coaching on how to adapt speech in formal and informal circumstances such as when speaking to a parent, teacher, playmate, or sibling.

Improve Instruction

Continue Language Exposure

As a complement to teaching reading through storytelling and show-and-tell activities, teachers should continue to enhance young students' oral language skills. Shared book reading to groups of students using a series such as "Big Books" can be effective in encouraging children to talk about shared experience with written texts. Stories developed by the whole class in "round robin" style also strengthen oral language and written communication skills. Students can also take turns reading the stories to one another in pairs.

Develop Phonological and Phonemic Awareness

Language studies show that phonological awareness correlates strongly with increased reading ability. Phonological awareness refers to the ability of a person to perceive and process the sounds of language; this phonological awareness includes phonemic awareness, for example, understanding that the sound of the first letter distinguishes "cat" from "sat." Phonemic awareness is particularly important for learners of Western European languages, including English and the Romance languages, because these phonemes are represented by the alphabetic letters or combinations of letters of those languages. When students understand the individual phonemes, they more readily learn alphabetic principles (how letters are mapped onto phonemes) and therefore tend to recognize printed words quickly.

Develop Fluency and Comprehension

When students stumble over word recognition, they find it difficult to focus on the meaning of a text. When students are fluent readers, they read texts accurately, quickly, and with expression; they can devote more attention to deriving meaning. Fluency increases with reading practice to the point where the reader combines efficient word recognition with simultaneous construction of meaning. Reading of texts with high-frequency words encourages fluency if the texts are interesting and meaningful to the reader. Repeated reading and pairing readers promotes fluency through practice. Teachers assess reading fluency best by listening to students while they read aloud.

Enrich Vocabulary

With a rich vocabulary, students develop more sophisticated comprehension as well as skillfulness in their writing. Vocabulary instruction is best situated in the context of understanding a specific text or domain of knowledge, building upon what students already know. Vocabulary taught in isolation tends not to be retained or used by students. Encouraging students to use new words in everyday life as well as in writing will strengthen vocabulary acquisition and retention. Direct instruction of new vocabulary, presenting definitions, example usage, etymology, and so on in the context of reading comprehension of a specific text will strengthen word awareness and teach students how to learn new words for themselves. Repetition and multiple exposures to vocabulary words (i.e., through speaking, writing, listening, and reading) helps solidify students' knowledge of a word, promoting its ease of use in their own speech and writing.

Foster Comprehension

Comprehension involves constructing meaning from a specific text based on word knowledge, critical thinking, and reasoning. Readers increase their understanding of texts when they work to follow the line of reasoning developed through a sequence of thoughts or an outline. Successful readers reflect on their own understanding of a text while they read and actively work to overcome difficulties in comprehension. Reading comprehension improves after connecting new information to prior knowledge and personal interest, learning new vocabulary in the context of reading, summarizing main points, and making predictions and critiques regarding information presented in the text.

Provide Feedback and Progress Measures

Text comprehension is generally assessed through questions about main points and perspectives of the text. Sophisticated assessments tailor questions to the current level of mastery, giving more difficult questions to students who correctly answer basic questions. Students' responses may be spoken or written, multiple choice, short answers, or essays. Assessments for non-native speakers should consider concepts that will be unfamiliar and align with the material studied by the students. Assessments should invite students to think critically, problem-solve, reason, interpret, imagine, and hypothesize. Close-ended questions can serve as brief diagnostic tools but should not be the main method of assessment.

Increase Classroom Morale

Teachers and students share responsibility for creating an ethic of caring and a non-discriminatory, respectful atmosphere for learning in the classroom. Regardless of students' gender, race, ethnicity, culture, and socioeconomic status, the teacher should support students to work together productively and thoughtfully within the classroom, the school, and the broader community. Proficient teachers attend to the needs and emotions of students and provide cognitive enrichment. Effective teachers often demonstrate a cheerful disposition, friendliness, emotional maturity, sincerity, and care for students as individuals and as learners. When teachers show an awareness of students' prior knowledge and experiences and maintain collaborative partnerships with parents and families, they affirm students' cultural backgrounds and interests.

Effective teachers create positive learning experiences that treat mistakes as natural and offer many opportunities for students to work together, correct their own errors, and pursue their interests, increasing students' motivation and achievement. Teaching students to ask questions without fear of ridicule and to collaborate in small groups supports the learners' social and emotional growth.

TEACHING ADDITIONAL LANGUAGES

The research summarized below should be helpful in a variety of circumstances, but the major reason for including it here is to help American educators bring their students who are non-fluent speakers of English into mainstream English language.[5] Two key research recommendations for teaching English language learners in the classroom are to help them achieve comprehensible communication and independent language learning.

Improve Instruction

Aim for Genuine, Comprehensible Communication

Research suggests that language instruction should provide contexts for learning grammar using a "communicative competence" approach rather than teaching grammar in isolation. Such practice in natural discourse gives purpose to grammar drills, pronunciation practice, and word memorization. Additional language instruction should aim to reproduce naturally occurring language exchanges, both unpredictable and context-specific. While challenging, students must learn how to start, maintain, and end unscripted and spontaneous conversations. In addition to structured language drills, teachers should use open-ended language practice opportunities (that have more than one possible solution) which allow students to develop oral and written fluency. Materials should reflect natural language patterns rather than artificially construed, textbook type conversation. Teachers should also encourage extensive reading and writing in the target language. Students improve their use and application of language with positive reinforcement and specific feedback, first on communication skills, and second, on language forms.

Effective teachers adopt the following strategies to foster comprehensible communication:

---

[5]This section summarizes the UNESCO booklet by Judd, Tan, and Walberg (2001), *Teaching Additional Languages.*

- demonstrating linguistic and vocabulary patterns and explaining how such patterns are formed, when they are used, and their cultural implications;
- teaching students speech acts (such as agreeing/disagreeing, apologizing, complimenting, etc.);
- modeling ways to manage conversations—such as openings, interruptions, closings, and so forth—and strategies for round-about speaking when a specific word is unknown or not readily accessible;
- providing controlled practice so that students can feel comfortable using the patterns;
- inviting students to use language patterns relevant to their speaking needs, such as ordering in a restaurant, asking for directions, or inviting someone to a party; and
- offering positive feedback, correction for errors, and specific suggestions at the end of practice to reinforce successful and continued language use.

Develop Independent Language Use

Effective language teachers give students independence while they acquire new language skills; students benefit from independent and guided experimentation that reminds them of strategies to reduce anxiety, raise pertinent questions about difficult points, and demonstrate sensitivity to others in expressing language. Teachers can help students with strategies for word memorization, thinking about their own language use, and for guessing and checking word meaning. Specific recommended strategies are to:

- observe which learning strategies are effective for each student;
- directly instruct students on specific strategies for language independence;
- tune into students' feelings and find ways to reduce anxiety; and
- encourage students to share successful strategies with each other.

In addition, lectures, the media (radio, cinema, television, and online video), and face-to-face conversations enable students to learn to understand naturally spoken language.

Foster Immersion

Consistent with many other findings described in this book, "time on task" works powerfully. Few Americans attained fluency in other languages unless they learned them at home or lived in other countries with people who spoke the other languages most of the time. Unless students practice other languages almost exclusively in their classes and outside of school, they are unlikely to acquire fluency. This, of course, is easier said than done, and few adults can acquire mastery of a new language with respect to pronunciation and natural fluency.

TEACHING MATHEMATICS

The effective practices identified in research are a mixture of new and old teaching methods.[6] Many studies document the strong relationship between increased instructional time and higher achievement. Nevertheless, in the United States, the 1996 National Assessment of Educational Progress (NAEP) shows that 20% of eighth grade students received 30 minutes or less in mathematics instruction daily. Such data indicate that time spent on instruction needs to be increased, but other factors need to be taken into account as this time is increased.

Improve Instructional Delivery

The problem of the limited amount of time spent on mathematics instruction is compounded by ineffective instructional methods. For example, the same sample of eighth graders (National Assessment of Educational Progress, 1996) apparently spent over 90% of mathematics class time practicing routine procedures. Less than 10% of mathematics instruction in a representative sample of eighth grade U.S. classrooms offered students practice in applying procedures to new situations. Mathematics teachers in countries whose students achieve higher scores on international tests than do U.S. students devote much more time to having students solve problems.

Although research indicates the necessity of increasing instructional time in mathematics, it also suggests that the extra time needs to provide students with opportunities for both practicing computations and procedures and inventing solutions. Other areas where the quality of the instruction proved effective included texts, focusing on meaning, concepts, problem solving, finding intuitive solutions, and developing number sense.

Use Textbooks Judiciously

Research reviews of modern mathematics texts show that much of textbook content is repetitive, particularly in elementary and middle grades; even students receiving extended instruction may not, at times, be enhancing their skills in mathematics if instructors slavishly follow the textbook. Such repetition may be a factor in an analysis of U.S. students' performance

---

[6]This section is based on Grouws and Cebulla (2000), *Improving Student Achievement in Mathematics*.

on the Trends in International Mathematics and Science Study (TIMSS) test. Analysis of results found strong differences in achievement levels based on U.S. students' exposure to mathematics concepts. Other equity concerns supported by research findings relate to increasing opportunity to learn in mathematics among girls, who tend to be out-performed by boys in mathematics. Math instruction can be improved by:

- using textbooks judiciously and supplementing content and problem solving with new material;
- aligning the mathematics curriculum and instruction to desired outcomes in problem solving, number sense, proportional reasoning, and deductive reasoning; and
- implementing strategies that boost the confidence, opportunity to learn, and instructional expectations in mathematics among females and low-scoring learners.

Focus on Meaning

Increased mathematics achievement occurs when mathematics instruction emphasizes "meaning making" as opposed to rote computation or formula application without a broader purpose. Research on teaching for meaning suggests that teachers should:

- emphasize the mathematical meanings of ideas, including how the idea, concept, or skill connects with other mathematical ideas in multiple ways, logically and consistently;
- create contexts and opportunities for students to make meaning of mathematical principles, formulas, problems, and solutions;
- explicitly draw connections between mathematics and other subjects, such as physics and social sciences; and
- show respect for creativity in arriving at solutions.

Integrate Concepts, Skills, and Problem Solving

Conceptual understanding of mathematical principles, formulas, and models increases when students spend more time solving problems, which also increases opportunities for discovery, invention, and experimentation. To increase opportunities for invention, teachers should:

- frequently use non-routine problems;
- periodically introduce a lesson involving a new skill by posing it as a problem to be solved; and
- regularly allow students to build new knowledge based on their intuitive knowledge and informal procedures.

Students who develop conceptual knowledge early perform better on procedural knowledge assessments later on. Students with strong conceptual understanding can quickly develop new procedural knowledge and skills. Therefore, teaching both simultaneously appears most efficient. Further, research indicates that teachers do not have to first concentrate on skill development and then have students work on problem solving. Skills can be developed on an as-needed basis, in the context of doing problem solving, not separately. Some research shows that students who are initially drilled too much on isolated skills will have a harder time conceptualizing, interpreting, and applying the skills later on. In one study, using knowledge of only basic addition, students demonstrated how they can extend learning by developing informal algorithms for addition of larger numbers. Effective teachers of mathematics use students' informal and intuitive knowledge in other areas to develop useful problem-solving methods and applications of mathematical knowledge.

Encourage Intuitive Solutions

In both Japanese and American classrooms, students demonstrate accelerated mathematical achievement after using inventive solution methodology extensively during instruction. When teachers are aware of how students construct knowledge, demonstrate familiarity with intuitive solution methods used by students, and use this knowledge in instructional planning, they provide the foundation for increased student achievement. When teachers structure instruction around problems, allow students to interact when solving these problems, and provide opportunities for students to share their solution methods, students perform at higher levels. These achievement gains in inventive solution finding do not weaken achievement levels on standardized mathematics achievement tests, research studies show.

When students have enough opportunity to develop their own solution methods, they can better apply mathematical knowledge to new problem situations. By balancing work in small groups with whole-class instruction and presentations, teachers provide a motivating and productive context for managing the breadth and depth of mathematics content and problem-solving opportunities. One strategy successfully used in Japanese mathematics lessons is to assign an interesting mathematics problem to the whole class and circulate throughout the room to observe students working independently and in small groups to develop solutions while taking notes on students' strategies. When the students finish, the teacher calls on students to share their solutions (from basic to most advanced) while the teacher shares key findings, useful strategies, and areas for growth after students' presentations. When managed well, whole class discussion may inform planning, build public knowledge, and accelerate student retention and application of mathematical content when contradictions in problem-solving methodologies are addressed.

Develop Number Sense

Number sense refers to the intuitive understanding an individual has for number size and combinations, the capacity to estimate solutions, as well as the ability to work flexibly with numbers in problem situations in order to make reasonable judgments. Number sense should not be taught in isolation from problem solving. Strengthening students' number sense while teaching mathematical topics generally increases students' numerical understandings. Research studies indicate that over 90% of the computation conducted outside of the classroom uses mental computation only, without pencil and paper or a calculator. Even effective use of a calculator requires strong number sense in case numbers are entered incorrectly or functions misapplied.

TEACHING SCIENCE

The principles here reflect research-based strategies for teaching scientific inquiry and resulting scientific knowledge and should be considered along with general teaching practices summarized in the first section of this chapter.[7] The various instructional strategies described are effective in stimulating students' scientific knowledge of hypotheses, facts, laws, and theories.

Engage Prior Learning

Suit Lessons to Learners

Students' prior knowledge and experiences—shaped by their gender, ethnicity, socioeconomic status, culture, native language, and other factors—requires teachers to use different kinds of explicit instructional support which scaffolds what students bring to scientific inquiry. Questioning and monitoring by teachers and within peer groups helps mediate challenges and difficulties that arise.

Effective strategies include:

- pretests to help determine prior learning and thus plan appropriate lessons;
- use of concrete, manipulative materials and familiar events to guide students' experience with scientific phenomena and encourage active construction of abstract concepts;

---

[7]This section summarizes Staver's (2007) *Teaching Science.*

- diversity in questioning, blending high-level, low-level, open-ended, and closed-ended questions;
- wait time of at least 3 seconds after asking a question before rephrasing it;
- wait time of at least 3 seconds following a student's response to a question before continuing; and
- setting the barometer of instructional difficulty slightly beyond one individual's capacity and within reach of the group's abilities.

Confront Conflicting Information

When students perceive a conflict between their prior knowledge and scientific knowledge, teachers can use the conflict as an opportunity to demonstrate empirical testing of concepts and openness to understanding new empirical knowledge. As advancements occur in our knowledge and interpretation of the solar system, in the concept of evolution, or in genetic engineering, for example, students have the chance to trace research and logical processes used to derive new scientific theories and discoveries.

Students benefit when teachers:

- show sensitivity to students' verbal and non-verbal behavior when presenting content that students may perceive as controversial;
- clarify the difference between understanding and believing;
- avoid using words such as "true" and "believe" in reference to scientific concepts;
- use peer-group discussions to guide enrichment in student thinking;
- concentrate upon testing predictions and making logical explanations based on raw data; and
- encourage students to think through how scientific concepts and theories benefit individuals, society, and the environment.

Coordinate Subjects Across Grade Level

Effective science teachers work collaboratively to align curricula and instruction with rigorous science standards. Science teaching produces higher levels of achievement when instructors:

- identify core ideas of the scientific discipline across all grade levels;
- decide on the scope and sequence of core scientific ideas to be taught in early, middle, and upper grades;
- outline the introduction of core scientific ideas in early grades and the process of elaboration in middle and upper grades;

- select science curricula for each grade level that develop core scientific knowledge and includes practice of independent scientific inquiry;
- select science curricula that emphasize scientific inquiry in instructional methods; and
- maintain strong consistency between goals and objectives of science content, instruction, and assessment for each lesson, unit, course, and program.

Motivate Students to Learn

Connect Science and Life

Students' motivation for scientific inquiry increases when science instruction builds upon students' interests, personal lives, societal issues, cultural backgrounds, and other school subjects. Deepened engagement with scientific inquiry occurs when students relate their new knowledge to things that are already meaningful and familiar. Teachers can relate new learning about science concepts and processes by

- connecting instructional plans explicitly to students' personal experiences;
- using examples and analogies;
- planning lessons to emphasize science, technology, and social concerns;
- providing students with opportunities to organize data into diagrams, tables, and graphs;
- encouraging students to use data from tables and graphs for pattern identification and predictions;
- helping students use mathematical operations, fractions, decimals, and percentages to calculate results of investigations;
- relating the concepts taught to science texts, and summarizing readings; and
- giving students the stage to role play scenes as scientific thinkers, inventors, or engineers.

Encourage Active Thinking

Teaching that encourages active knowledge construction through scientific inquiry and experimentation generates learner interest and achievement. To maximize proactive scientific inquiry, teachers

- present science as a process of constructing and empirically testing models for their ability to explain and predict scientific phenomena;

- spend time diagnosing students' alternative conceptions;
- use a variety of teaching approaches from open and guided inquiry to direct instruction;
- align instructional strategies and assessment with each lesson's content goals;
- employ methods that assist students in their identifying inconsistencies in reasoning and facts;
- deliberately raise students' awareness of how they construct knowledge both individually and together;
- consider interdependent relationships of scientific concepts when sequencing instruction of them;
- demonstrate engagement with scientific concepts through use of discrepant events;
- use familiar analogies and physical models to guide students to thoughtful conclusions;
- adapt curricula and instructional strategies to best suit diverse needs of individual students, small groups, and whole group; and
- conduct frequent assessments to guide new teaching and modification of instruction.

Establish High Expectations

Students set their own expectations for learning with modeling from teachers. Teachers' expectations influence the path of student behavior and achievement through verbal and nonverbal interactions with students, such as praise, smiling affirmation, eye contact, nodding, and time spent on interactions. When teachers spend the time to notice changes in students' level of mastery and adjust the difficulty of the instructional task, students tend to respond by increasing their motivation and persistence to master new material. When low ability is perceived as a fixed attribute, teachers can foster new beliefs in the benefits of continued effort and practice.

Effective science teachers:

- monitor and analyze students' work and take corrective action with each individual and group as needed;
- instill confidence in students by incremental affirmations of their efforts, progress, and lessons learned;
- increase students' capacity and confidence by dividing difficult tasks into small steps that seem manageable and achievable;
- offer assistance, but do not do the students' work for them;
- offer students' choices and some control over their own learning;
- facilitate opportunities to celebrate successful achievement of small and large milestones; and

- reinforce the value of persistence as students experience difficulties or setbacks.

Deepen the Learning Experience

Questioning and problem solving promote deepened understanding of scientific concepts. When an individual does not know how to proceed to the desired answer, the challenge is to solve problems using concepts, reflection, and qualitative strategies. Even when it depends largely upon mathematics, problem solving improves with pictures, diagrams, and other qualitative methods. Effective problem solvers demonstrate detailed representations of a problem, organize a relevant knowledge base, plan solutions to the problem, and enact strategies to identify and correct errors.

Scientific understanding begins when teachers:

- ask all students if they have a good-to-excellent idea or little-to-no idea how to do specific tasks to determine the degree of problem solving involved to complete an exercise;
- organize cooperative student groups that reflect intellectual, gender, and cultural diversity and foster opportunities for group members to share representations of the knowledge gap and proposed solution strategies;
- use guided inquiry to lead students to new knowledge;
- aim problem-solving instruction just beyond what learners can do on their own, but within parameters of what can be achieved with assistance;
- use science concepts and processes as basis for students to write, speak, interpret data, and apply mathematics;
- design discussions and negotiations among students as a regular part of scientific inquiry; and
- offer students opportunities to claim ownership over their learning.

Thus, as illustrated in this chapter, some general evidence-based principles of teaching can be justified. In addition, some teaching principles with respect to the conditions and subjects of school are sufficiently evidenced to recommend.

CHAPTER 5

SCHOOLS

This chapter illustrates the parallels in student learning, parent childrearing, and classroom practices described in Chapters 2 through 4, with practices carried out in the school as a whole. Those responsible—parents, teachers, and principals—can cooperate in sustaining large amounts of highly engaged student learning. Though teamwork is important for success, the school administration, chiefly the principal, is actually or nominally responsible for leadership. As illustrated in subsequent chapters, the policies of school districts and states can also facilitate school practices and leadership described in this chapter.

Increase Opportunity to Learn and Class Time

In a synthesis of research on *school*-level effects on learning, Marzano (2000) found the most influential indicator to be the "opportunity to learn," which he defines as the extent to which curriculum, instruction, and testing are aligned with standards (see Table 2). Coinciding with classroom- and student-level research as discussed in previous chapters, Marzano further identifies class time as the second most influential of the school-level influences.

Improving Student Learning: Action Principles for Families, Classrooms, Schools, Districts, and States, pages 59–71

TABLE 2. School-Level Influences on Student Learning

Variable	Relative Effect
Opportunity to Learn	.88
Class Time	.39

Note: From *A New Era of School Reform: Going Where Research Takes Us,* by R. Marzano (2000, p. 56). Aurora, CO: Mid-Continent Research for Education and Learning.

Employ Effective Schools Practices

The Education Trust (Jerald, 2001) reports that in 47 states and the District of Columbia, effective education policies and teaching practices enabled more than 4,500 high-poverty and high-minority schools (high meaning over 50%) to perform among the top one third of schools in their states and often to outperform predominantly White schools in advantaged communities. These schools educate about 1,280,000 low-income students, about 564,000 African American students, and about 660,000 Latino students (the groups overlap).

Such research findings by the Education Trust corroborate research syntheses of control-group research and large-scale analyses of surveys. Principals of these high-achieving schools with students from predominantly minority and high-poverty backgrounds report a number of common features of their schools. Similarly, based on extensive research and field-testing, Goldring, Porter, Murphy, Elliot, and Cravens (2007) developed a set of indicators of principal effectiveness subsequently discussed. Their indicators have much in common with the features reported by Jerald (2001) discussed below.

A synthesis of 17 such studies of high-poverty schools (Center for Public Education, 2009) showed ten factors that distinguished high-performing schools from others:

- a culture of high expectations and caring for students;
- a safe and disciplined environment;
- a principal who is a strong instructional leader;
- hard-working teachers dedicated to student learning;
- a curriculum focused on academic achievement that emphasizes basic skills and literacy;
- increased instructional time;
- ongoing, diagnostic assessment;
- parents as partners in learning;
- professional development to improve student achievement; and
- collaboration among teachers and other staff.

Align Content to Standards

In his research synthesis, Jerald (2001) found that successful schools make extensive use of state and local standards to design curriculum, instruction, and assessment of student work. This practice ensures that for students who progress in school, instruction can be coordinated across the curriculum for maximum impact, and that similar instruction will not be needlessly repeated at the expense of new learning. This approach requires collaboration among teachers at the same grade level and among grade levels, and such collaboration must be supported by school leaders. Goldring and others (2007) identified a conceptual framework of principal effectiveness in which setting high standards—with rigorous individual, team, and school goals for academic and social learning—served as a key indicator of probable achievement gains.

Provide Challenging, Well-Defined Student Goals

Nearly all studies carried out in a wide variety of industries and firms show that setting specific, challenging goals lead to higher performance than setting easy, "do-your-best," or no goals, that is, no pressure to achieve. Goals affect performance by

- directing attention;
- mobilizing effort;
- increasing persistence; and
- motivating strategy development.

Goal setting is most likely to improve task performance when the goals are specific and sufficiently challenging, feedback is provided, the experimenter or manager is supportive, and the assigned goals are accepted by the individual (Lock, Shaw, Saari, & Latham, 1981). Thus, schools should establish a goal-oriented ethos, an ethos that can be established by administrators and teacher leaders and communicated to students, both as individuals and as groups, and to their parents. School leaders can help create this goal-oriented culture by involving the whole school population in a worthwhile but modest joint beginning project that can provide a model of successfully achieving goals for both classrooms and individuals.

Offer Student Incentives

Student incentives, particularly those aligned with high curriculum standards, promote learning and provide a complementary strategy to setting specific learning goals. Elementary school children can benefit from encouragement, praise, feedback about accomplishments, and other non-monetary reinforcement.

Because of the allure of adolescent peer groups, middle grade students can be constructively motivated by the threat of grade retention. An example is Chicago's Summer Bridge program. Parents and students chose between grade retention or passing a demanding examination at the end of intensive remediation courses over the summer. Over the short summer session, the program showed increases in reading and math scores comparable to one half to a year of instruction, depending on subject and grade level. Notably, the lowest achievers gained the most, and the students were able to maintain those gains over the following years, making the program exceptionally effective while requiring relatively little time and money (Betts & Costrell, 2001).

It is usually assumed that adults in the (non-unionized) workforce perform better if they are offered bonuses and raises. It might be expected that older students would also be constructively influenced by monetary incentives. Bishop's (1996) large-scale, statistically controlled study strongly suggested that the New York Regents' policy of awarding college scholarships to high school students based on their scores on a rigorous, end-of-high-school examination served to increase student achievement in the state. Similarly, as discussed in Chapter 2, the O'Donnell Foundation's $100 payment to both teachers and students for each (college-credited) Advanced Placement examination raised the numbers of passing students twelve-fold in inner-city Dallas high schools (Jackson, 2008; Walberg, 1998). Such incentive programs are now being instituted in schools in the United States and other countries.

AMOUNT AND QUALITY OF INSTRUCTION

Increase Learning Time

Jerald (2001) found that principals of high-achieving schools in challenging socioeconomic circumstances attribute their performance to increased instruction time for reading and mathematics. Corroborating control-group research and analyses of national surveys show that the effects of the amount of homework teachers require each week, thus extending learning time, are significant. Indeed, mathematics homework proved to be a more important determinant of gains in achievement than any of the standard measures of school quality, such as teacher education and experience or class size (Betts & Costrell, 2001).

A recent synthesis on the positive effects of homework, particularly in upper grades, extends these earlier research syntheses and findings (Cooper, Robinson, & Patall, 2006). The incentive effect of homework appears enhanced when it is commented on and graded (Walberg, 2006).

Provide Effective Instruction

In addition to effective methods of classroom teaching discussed in Chapters 2 and 4, the positive effects have been observed at the school level. Quality of instruction includes both the content and the instructional experience. Among their set of indicators of principal effectiveness, Goldring and others (2007) identified giving students access to detailed curriculum content in core academic subjects as one feature of schools where the behavior of leaders might be emulated. Their schools also were characterized by successful instructional methods that got the most out of student learning.

According to Jerald (2001), such high-quality instruction necessitates the use of assessments to help guide instruction as a healthy part of everyday teaching and learning. Such high-quality instruction also requires, especially in disadvantaged schools, high-quality professional development for teachers. Moreover, that professional development should focus on instructional practices that help students meet academic standards. Teachers' evaluations of the professional development they receive may help improve what is offered. In short, successful school leaders insist on performance accountability and set high performance standards for themselves and for their teachers, including individual and collective responsibility among the professional staff.

Grade Students in Accord with Their Mastery

Complementary to setting goals to motivate students and insisting on accountability, tough grading standards are an aspect of the quality of instruction and benefit learning. Such policies work best when expectations are widely shared throughout the school so that some students do not perceive differences as inequitable or onerous compared to what is required of their peers. Requiring high-quality work for a given assigned grade generally raises achievement, particularly for high-achieving students who might not otherwise be sufficiently challenged.

Monitor Response to Intervention

As suggested above, tough grading standards go hand-in-hand with a comprehensive system to monitor individual student performance and to provide help to struggling students before they fall behind (Jerald, 2001). A special education term, "response to intervention" (RTI) means to systematically identify and remediate learning difficulties and applies directly to the necessity of monitoring student progress. Some students may fail to progress under a regime of regular classroom teaching. They may require both special diagnosis and special remediation of their specific problems, which may include a lack of prerequisite knowledge and skills—that is, prior learning—or one of the various forms of disabilities. RTI is similar to "mastery learning" in which students who fail at part of a lesson are given more time or alternative instruction to help them catch up with others. RTI has grown mightily because of the huge rise of students classified as needing special education programs.

Since the Individuals with Disabilities Act (IDEA) in 1975, the number and percentage of youths ages 3–21 receiving special education services greatly increased. In 1976–77, IDEA served 3.7 million youth, comprising up to 8% of total public school enrollment. By 2005–06, the number increased to about 6.7 million youth receiving IDEA services, an 81% growth in numbers, corresponding to 14% of total public school enrollment (U.S. Department of Education, National Center for Education Statistics, 2007). The most rapidly growing disability is classified as a "specific learning disability," which

> involves one or more of the basic psychological processes involved in understanding or in using language, spoken or written, that may manifest itself in an imperfect ability to listen, think, speak, read, write, spell, or to do mathematical calculations, including conditions such as perceptual disabilities, brain injury, minimal brain dysfunction, dyslexia, and developmental aphasia. (U.S. Department of Education, National Center for Education Statistics, 2007, Indicator 7)

From 1976–77 through 2005–06, the percentage of youths, aged 3–21, receiving special education services for a specific learning disability increased threefold (from 2% to 6% of enrolled youth). The rise of RTI can be attributed to two assessments that proved unhelpful—school readiness assessments and IQ-achievement discrepancies.

School readiness assessments are intended to identify children likely to have a specific learning disability. More than one third of states require kindergarten screenings (Cannella & Reiff, 1989), which involve tests of pre-academic skills including motor, cognitive, perceptual, sensory, and social behaviors. Children who fail the screenings may be placed in transition classes or asked to wait another year before starting kindergarten (Meisels, 1999). The Individuals with Disabilities Act of 2004 allows school districts to use up to 15% of special education funds to finance early intervention activities.

A synthesis of 70 longitudinal studies showed that school readiness assessments crudely predict achievement in the early grades (LaParo & Pianta, 2000). The authors concluded that "the results from early assessments make, at best, only small to moderate contributions to the predictability of children's early school success" (LaParo & Pianta, 2000, p. 475). Among the reasons that readiness assessments lack much predictive validity are that young children are difficult to assess, achievement tests in the early grades lack reliability, and that presumed deficits may wax and wane.

A second diagnostic assessment that has not fulfilled its promise is the measurement of the discrepancy between low achievement and relatively high IQ or general ability. Discrepancy assessments entail considerable measurement error, reflect possible biases of IQ tests, and lack suggestions for specific interventions aligned with student needs and explicit achievement standards.

Response to intervention, on the other hand, emphasizes prevention rather than allowing students to fall far behind before providing tailored remediation. Thus, RTI provides individually appropriate instruction, or intervention, monitors the learning rate over time, and provides additional remediation as necessary. Such close attention to each student's progress is likely to require a carefully planned, often computer-based system for tracking each student's progress with respect to the attainment of short-term goals and long-term standards.

Act on Response to Intervention

The origins of RTI have been attributed to Deno's data-based "curriculum-based measurement" (CBM) to plan and evaluate instruction and Bergan's behavioral (i.e., problem-solving) consultation model, both emphasizing core components of what would become identified as RTI (Bergan, 1977; Bergan & Kratochwill, 1990; Deno, 1985; Deno & Mirkin, 1977). This earlier research has been elaborated on by many researchers as well as educators that champion RTI (also known as the Problem Solving Model), in an attempt to adopt scientific assessment–intervention methods for improving students' achievement. Generally, the features of CBM are direct measurement, repeated measurement, and time series analysis.

Ongoing data collection and analysis of student performance is a critical component of the RTI method, and CBM appears superior to the usual commercial tests in demonstrating validity and reliability in evaluating student growth, providing data to make instructional changes, setting goals for students, and predicting performance on high-stakes tests (Education Evolving, 2005). More than 400 studies have been published on the technical adequacy and use of CBM (Espin & Wallace, 2004), which provides the type of dynamic, specific, and generative data required for RTI, such that practitioners can make effective classification and placement decisions.

Program variants of RTI have up to four tiers of instruction (Ikeda & Gustafson, 2002, as cited in Fuchs & Fuchs, 2006). Actions at each level are as follows:

Level 1: The teacher confers with student's parent(s) to work on resolving the academic or behavioral problems.

Level 2: The teacher and the school's building assistance team convene to identify and analyze problems and help the teacher select, implement, and monitor the effectiveness of an intervention.

Level 3: Staff use behavioral problem solving to refine or redesign the intervention and coordinate its implementation.

Level 4: Specialists provide special education assistance and due process protections.

At each level, instructional intensity for lagging students increases through several means:

- using more teacher-centered, systematic, and explicit or scripted instruction;
- conducting instruction more frequently;
- adding to the time duration;
- creating smaller and more homogeneous groupings; and
- relying on instructors with greater expertise.

Velluntino and others (1996) describe other RTI models that deserve consideration.

A synthesis of 14 empirical studies of RTI variants (Coleman, Buysse, & Neizel, 2006) revealed an emerging body of empirical evidence to support claims that RTI is "an effective method for identifying children at risk for learning difficulties and for providing specialized interventions either to ameliorate or to prevent the occurrence of learning disabilities" (pp. 26–27). Children maintained achievement gains through the first part of first grade, based on this review of research on RTI. This evidence suggests that early interventions provide maximum benefit. While this research concentrates on the impact of RTI for language and literacy development, much less is known about RTI's effectiveness for mathematics, social and emotional development, student behavior, and other precursors of learning issues identified among younger children, including language delays, attention, and self-regulation.

No evidence suggests that RTI would be ineffective for other students including those that are able and older. Indeed, RTI is similar to mastery learning, which has a strong, consistent record of achievement success (Walberg, 1983, 2006). Some common elements are frequent assessments of achievement progress, and, for laggards, alternate methods and increased amounts of instruction.

ORGANIZING SCHOOLS

In a rare 15-year longitudinal study, Bryk, Sebring, Allensworth, Leppescu, and Easton (2009) studied the features of schools in Chicago associated with sustained student achievement gains. Five organizational principles differentiated successful schools from others. Condensed, these are:

- Employ coherent, ambitious instruction
- Build professional capacity
- Strengthen parent-community ties
- Use school leadership as a driver of change
- Foster a positive learning environment

SOCIAL AND EMOTIONAL LEARNING

Goldring and others (2007) posit that a robust school culture where the priority is on student learning is a key indicator of principal effectiveness and that social learning, too, is evidenced in well-run schools. In fact, five of six of the indicators of principal effectiveness identified by Goldring and her colleagues include social learning along with academic learning as a feature of effective schools (see section below).

*Begin Academically Focused Social and Emotional Learning
Programs*

Social and emotional learning (SEL) enhances students' ability to integrate thinking, feeling, and behavior to achieve academic and life tasks (Elias, 2003). Typically, social and emotional learning programs are instituted as part of a school-wide effort that requires the cooperation and support of school staff and, ideally, parents and the community as well. They provide direct instruction and experience in learning about oneself and getting along well with others, primarily to foster school achievement and responsible behavior. The programs potentially influence primary outcomes such as:

- successfully mastering subject matter;
- sustaining motivation to continue learning;
- improving student attitudes toward an interest in school;

- fostering academically engaged time;
- enhancing bonding to school;
- reducing suspensions, expulsions, and grade retentions;
- improving attendance and graduation rates;
- building peer leadership skills; and
- achieving constructive employment.

Improved social and emotional learning can also benefit secondary outcomes, including improved self-efficacy and cooperation; abstention from delinquency; development of social skills and problem solving; better effort and self-regulation; increased attributions of perceived control; community bonding; healthier living, including decreased substance abuse; decreased interpersonal violence; and more constructive family life.

Identify Appropriate Social and Emotional Learning Programs

The non-profit Collaborative for Academic, Social, and Emotional Learning (CASEL) identified a comprehensive, research-based compilation of essential social and emotional skills that support effective performance in academic and life tasks. This compilation can be used to guide the development of academic assignments, projects, tests, homework, and lesson planning.[1] Schools that reinforce the development of these skills give students improved opportunities for stronger academic performance. Furthermore, the CASEL (2003) publication, *Safe and Sound*, provides "reviews [of] 80 multiyear, sequenced SEL programs designed for use in general education classrooms" to help educational leaders identify programs that suit the specific needs of their districts and schools.[2]

Link Social and Emotional Activities to School Programs

Children benefit from coordinated, explicit, developmentally sensitive instruction in the prevention of specific problems such as smoking, drug use, alcohol consumption, early pregnancy, violence, and bullying. Constructive eating habits, healthy sleeping patterns, and disciplined study regimens and work environments promote academic, social, and emotional learning.

---

[1] The CASEL compilation is conveniently summarized by Elias (2003) in the UNESCO pamphlet, *Academic and Social-Emotional Learning.*

[2] *Safe and Sound* is free and downloadable at http://www.casel.org/programs/selecting.php; new and promising programs are also listed on that webpage.

Age-appropriate conflict resolution techniques help students make more constructive choices, particularly when taking into account students' culture, disabilities, and other individual and contextual factors. Administrators should allocate time in the school curriculum to address appropriate health issues and behavioral problem prevention among students and staff. Guidance and counseling services should be available to help students on an ongoing basis to confront difficult situations.

Promote Community Service to Build Empathy

In addition to providing a goal-oriented model for in-school academic work, as discussed above, community service projects foster a connection to social causes among students. Even at young ages, students benefit from community service by feeling they are making a contribution. Service experiences usually help students to encounter other people, ideas, and circumstances in ways that broaden their worldview and build empathetic understanding, but they should not reduce study time.

Meaningful participation in the larger community and world around them helps prepare children for their eventual roles in larger society, their families, and work groups. Examples of projects include improving the physical environment around the school, helping the elderly, and providing comfort to the injured or sick. Students should be prepared for the type of circumstances they will face, have safe direct involvement in the tasks appropriate to their age, take time to process their reflections in speech or writing, and share their reflections with others.

Build Social and Emotional Skills Systemically and Cumulatively

Social and emotional learning programs should be implemented with thoughtful consideration of local needs, goals, interests, and mandates; staff skills, workload, and receptiveness; pre-existing instructional efforts and activities; the content and quality of program materials, as well as their developmental and cultural appropriateness to the students; and the wants of parents and community members. After 2 or 3 years of practice and trial implementation, staff can more effectively align the program with state and national educational standards, comply with legal standards and mandates, and obtain necessary support from administration and community. Social and emotional learning should be reinforced through subject areas to foster deeper understanding of the content and minimize behavior disruptions. Students thrive academically, socially, and emotionally when given a degree of autonomy over the content, methods, and environment in which they learn. When teachers and other adults listen to students' needs and preferences, the result is a more responsive and productive learning environment.

PARENT RELATIONS

As indicated in Chapter 3, parents are important cultivators of the academic development of their children. Jerald (2001) finds that school-wide parental involvement in efforts to get students to meet standards is a key feature of high-achieving schools that succeed in spite of limited resources attributable to socioeconomic status.

Initiate School-Parent Programs

Families also are a key to providing support for the academic, social, and emotional learning of their children, and school leaders and teachers can help foster this development through outreach to parents, including welcoming parents to the school. Parents should have overviews of current lessons for their children reinforcing academic skills. Displays of students' work encourages parents to affirm their children's efforts, and inviting parents to join classroom activities and do family-oriented instructional projects creates alignment between a child's academic and home life.

Parents benefit, moreover, from opportunities for guidance and networking with other parents on how to raise their children effectively, such as developing healthy morning and homework routines that aid children in achieving required goals. The book *Emotionally Intelligent Parenting* (Elias, Tobias, & Friedlander, 2000) offers useful insights and strategies for parents. A practical guide for parent education and programs for academic success is free for downloading (Redding, 2000). Many useful research and practical articles may also be found in the *School Community Journal* (www. adi.org) for free download.

PRINCIPALS AS INSTRUCTIONAL LEADERS

Establishing a goal-oriented school ethos, creating an aligned, rigorous core curriculum delivered with quality instruction, ensuring teachers devote sufficient time to their students' learning in core subjects and intervening with those students who need help, and establishing a school and home culture that encourages effective, lasting academic, social, and emotional learning are all aspects of the ways schools—and their leaders—can improve outcomes for children. In those schools where the core indicators of principal effectiveness were achieved, Goldring and others (2007) observed a number of key behaviors among effective principals. They are condensed here as follows:

- Plan coherent activities for realizing high standards
- Engage people and resources to realize high standards
- Support enabling activities for academic and social learning
- Advocate for the needs of students within and beyond the school
- Communicate with staff and community members
- Systematically collect and analyze data to guide decisions.

In addition, to achieve these operational goals, principals and other school leaders can provide professional development for teachers, especially professional development focused on instructional practices to help students meet academic standards (Jerald, 2001). Thus, as illustrated in this chapter, several principles of successful schooling encourage and reinforce effective teaching practices. Others parallel classroom teaching principles.

CHAPTER 6

DISTRICTS

Though traditional educators may disagree with the trends, many citizens, legislators, business people, and parents want higher and more uniform standards and corresponding examinations to measure progress and compare schools. Because of these wants and because of NCLB, the states are responding with objective measures of achievement. In turn, districts and schools are increasingly aligning instruction with the state standards, providing student incentives, and, through Response to Intervention, adapting instruction to what individual students need to succeed. Though less definitive than that described in other parts of this book, research on leadership and local policies yields a number of common sense principles that are in accord with expert and some educators' views and that seem possible to put in practice, as discussed in this chapter.

This chapter and the next depart from the preceding chapters in that they do not focus on the direct elements of learning and education practices. Rather, local and state policies have indirect or "distal" influences on learning, compared with the more direct or "proximal" influences of teaching, student engagement, and parental support. Even so, recent research shows that some district and state policies improve student outcomes, such as incentives and sanctions through accountability policies, expanded choice options, and policy support for improved classroom instruction.

And it is with the latter, policies that improve teaching, that this chapter is most concerned.

EFFECTIVE DISTRICT EDUCATIONAL POLICIES

Dailey, Fleischman, Gil, Holtzman, O'Day, and Vosmer (2005) asked, "What does it take to achieve high-performing school districts, particularly those serving low-income children" (p. 1). To answer this question, Dailey and others (2005) analyzed 19 documents based on the knowledge of experts and insights from experienced practitioners. As the authors declare, their findings are not definitive, because they are not based on rigorous research studies, as in the case of many of the other findings in this book. Even so, they accord well with research findings on teachers and principals, and given the paucity of rigorous research, professional and expert opinion is worth considering. According to their assessment, the seven (abbreviated) themes characterize high-performing districts:

- Focus on student achievement and learning;
- Work from a plan of clear goals and improvements;
- Commit to professional learning opportunities;
- Use data to guide improvement;
- Enact comprehensive, coherent reform policies;
- Require educators to accept responsibility for student learning;
- Provide educators with helpful support; and
- Monitor programs regularly and intervene if necessary.

THE TEACHING FORCE

Aside from parents and students themselves, teachers are directly responsible for how much students learn in school, and Chapter 4 is devoted to describing effective teaching principles. A good teacher can have effects that continue to be influential in subsequent grades and even in adult life. Unfortunately, despite centuries of teaching, the recruitment and selection of effective teachers is only now being scientifically documented, but moderate progress has been made in the last decade.

District offices are the initial routes to employment for most teachers. Although many school districts have begun experimenting with various forms of school-based hiring in order to select teachers deemed more likely to fit the specific needs and environment of the specific school, districts may still prescreen teacher candidates for site-based hiring. Furthermore, it is the district that typically sets the parameters for school-based hiring, and it is typically the district with whom public school teachers typically contract, whatever their route to employment may be. Because of their continuing central role in hiring teachers and the crucial importance of the teacher in student learning, this chapter on districts describes the best ways to recruit, select, and pay teachers.

Employ Well-Educated, Knowledgeable Teachers

Barber and Mourshed (2007) studied 25 economically advanced countries to discover what parts of their elementary and secondary school systems made for high performance on international achievement assessments. In high-performing countries education was greatly valued, which led some of the most able undergraduates to pursue teaching. Education officials could hire from a large number of highly qualified candidates with the highest academic qualifications. U.S. research bears out Barber and Mourshed's conclusion. A recent research synthesis showed that teacher selectivity benefits student performance (Wayne & Youngs, 2003). Among 21 studies qualifying for inclusion in the synthesis, the college and university rigor, test scores, rigorous subject matter courses, and academic degrees showed such effects.

Despite the critical significance of quality teachers for student outcomes, efforts to improve the teaching work force in the United States leave considerable room for improvement. *Education Week's* "Quality Counts 2008" grades states across six areas of education performance and policy. In the area of teaching improvement (which includes state efforts to increase accountability, provide incentives for talented people to enter and stay in the profession, monitor and allocate the distribution of talent, and build the capacity of teachers and principals to improve student learning), states earned a "C" on average.

The "Quality Counts 2008" survey shows that states increasingly require prospective teachers to have a major or its equivalent in the subjects they plan to teach and to pass tests of basic skills and subject matter to earn a teaching license. Even so, districts commonly fail to meet such hiring requirements, particularly in mathematics and science, and the state examinations measure basic rather than advanced knowledge and skills.

Similarly, states are lax in ensuring the quality of their teacher preparation programs, although the situation is improving. Thirty states rate their teacher preparation programs based on the percentage of their graduates who pass state licensing exams, and 18 states hold teacher preparation programs accountable for the classroom performance of their graduates. Districts, of course, can circumvent weak state requirements and low standards by requiring higher qualifications.

Employ Valid Screening Tests

Since the usual teacher qualifications are still lax, researchers have conducted voluminous statistical research to identify predicatively valid qualifications. In retrospect, the results seem obvious: the best indicator of potential teaching success is knowledge of the subject. It stands to reason that teachers can't teach what they don't know, and, moreover, that a deep command of the subject allows them to make confident presentations and answer in depth unexpected student questions. In addition, some teaching methods (documented in previous chapters) have proven records of success. As in other professions, it is now possible to validly measure the professional skills and subject knowledge of teachers and for districts to require both pedagogical proficiency and subject matter mastery when selecting teachers.

The American Board for the Certification of Teacher Excellence (ABCTE) has done just this. Supported with approximately $46 million in grants from the U.S. Department of Education, it has not only developed such examinations but also demonstrated that those who pass teach more effectively by the criterion of student achievement gains. Based on its examinations, it now offers the Passport to Teaching alternative teacher certification program (valid in seven states), a reading certificate program, and licenses in elementary education (K–6), English/language arts (6–12), mathematics (6–12), general science (6–12), biology (6–12), physics (6–12), chemistry (6–12), and special education (K–12). The licensing system is called Passport to Teaching because passing the examination allows teaching entry and transfer in multiple states.

A study of the Passport to Teaching certification program (Boots, 2007) shows that current teachers who would have earned certification through this alternative certification route by passing the examination increased student outcomes more than teachers who would have failed. In Tennessee, a section of fourth- through sixth-grade teachers took the two ABCTE examinations needed for elementary certification, which are the Professional Teaching Knowledge exam and the Multiple Subject Exam. This research showed a direct correlation of teacher performance on the ABCTE mathematics and professional knowledge examinations with student mathematics achievement gains, based on teacher-linked student achievement data of the Tennessee Value-Added Assessment System.

An independent study of the ABCTE Passport certificate holders who have classroom teaching positions showed their principals rated them as "more effective" or "somewhat more than effective" than "all other teachers [they had] observed in their career" on every dimension (Glazerman, Tuttle, & Baxter, 2006, p. 3). This research is the first report in a 5-year, independent longitudinal evaluation of ABCTE certification programs, which has randomly assigned students to teachers having earned the Passport to Teaching certificate and to other teachers who have not, for perhaps the most rigorous evaluation ever conducted of a professional examination system.

The ABCTE can facilitate the selection of more knowledgeable teachers as well as enlarge the pool of desirable candidates. The Tarrance Group (2007) poll of Florida residents revealed that 82% believed that "someone with several years of real-world experience in the subject they want to teach, who knows the strategies of excellent teaching but has never taught before," (p. 1) would make a good teacher. Of college educated adults, almost 3 out of 10 would think about a career in education if they didn't have to take an additional year or two of education courses to become certified.

It should be emphasized that ABCTE does not promise to select effective teachers but, as in other professional licensing, to guarantee that beginners and experienced teachers have required professional knowledge, in this case of the subject to be taught and how to teach it. Fortunately, it is turning out that teachers who demonstrate this knowledge help their students learn more than those without such demonstrated knowledge, which confirms previous research of the validity of the criteria.

Pay Teachers for Performance

The Education Week's "Quality Counts 2008" survey shows that states rarely ensure rigorous, regular evaluations of teachers' on-the-job performance. Though 43 states require formal evaluations for all teachers, only 26 states require formal training for individuals conducting the evaluations. Only a dozen require annual teacher evaluations.

Because of tenure and tradition, there may be little reason for serious, systematic evaluation if teachers are given no incentives or other reasons to perform well. The professions of law and medicine are often paid by clients, which gives them a strong incentive to perform well or, at least, to their clients' satisfaction. Unlike K–12 teaching, in many other professions and occupations, pay is at least partially related to merit or performance.

Instead, nearly all teachers are paid according to a "single-salary schedule" or "position-automatic system," which means that, within a district, all teachers with a given number of years of experience and education level are paid identically. Except for the first few years of teaching, neither of these pay determinants is linked to student achievement. Even special pay for hard-to-recruit subjects such as science and mathematics and "combat pay" for teaching in difficult schools are rare. The exception is private and charter schools in which performance pay is more common.

Such uniformity does not follow the fundamental, commonsense principle of economics and behavioral psychology that appropriate incentives affect behavior. Of course, the incentives may not necessarily be monetary. In contrast to economists, industrial psychologists emphasize praise and other recognition, prestige of the organization, and attractive working conditions. They may also emphasize the obligation of team responsibilities—playing fair, and excelling as in sports competition—and intrinsic satisfaction from work well done. In efforts to improve performance, such conditions are employed by firms.

Even so, pay for performance is most often the chief consideration. Reviews of research show that performance pay usually yields positive effects on outcomes in private firms, federal government agencies, and teaching (Lazear & Shaw, 2007; Podgursky & Springer, 2007). In private firms, over three quarters of non-hourly employees are covered by pay-for-performance systems (Podgursky & Springer, 2007), and performance pay has been growing rapidly in the federal government (Nelson, 2008). To raise productivity further in firms, the percentage of "base pay" is shrinking, and the share of performance pay is increasing. Because of the continuing school crisis, policymakers are beginning to try increasing amounts of performance pay in K–12 education.

Of course, extreme pay spreads can induce extreme efforts but may also induce serious problems, such as cheating. Other problems of large pay spreads may include less cooperation among employees or even sabotage. A balanced choice may be necessary between the incentive inducement and possible adverse consequences, and it is the responsibility of managers to design and maintain optimal programs. Managers may find it unpleasant to evaluate and rank people who report to them, but if their own pay is incentivized, they may be more receptive to evaluating others.

On the other hand, technology may obviate such difficult managerial choices and their possibly adverse consequences. In the competitive marketplace, few musicians, artists, actors, and sportspeople can make a living at their forté but, by appearing on television, or using other media, a few can make millions of dollars a year. The world's best violinist becomes accessible. In such cases, markets decide the performance pay, consumers and the most appealing performers reap the benefits. The complications and uncertainties of group management are avoided.

An interesting example in education is high achieving Korea, which has a $15 billion per year, highly competitive for-profit *hogwan* tutoring industry with extensive brick-and-mortar facilities (Walberg, 2007b). Since 2000, however, the firm Megastudy has been offering web-based educational services and now boasts 2,000 courses. Teachers receive about a quarter of the subscription income to their lectures, which has added up to a payment of $2 million in a single recent year in the case of one charismatic English teacher. Such entrepreneurship and differential pay are nearly unheard of in Western public and private schools. Indeed, the lack of entrepreneurship and incentives may be a major reason for the low and declining productivity of American K–12 education.

In K–12 education, principals may be reluctant to rank the effectiveness of teachers since teachers may dislike being compared. Yet, research shows principal rankings are substantially correlated with the achievement progress of students under each teacher (Podgursky & Springer, 2007). Firms solve this problem by insisting on rankings, which disallow uniform "excellent" ratings, and compensating leaders themselves in part for their unit's progress. They may be given autonomy to assess, encourage, and compensate their staff members individually or collectively for group performance. (Splitting bonuses or merit raises equally among staff may avoid dissention but allows individual slacking—what personnel economists call "free riding.")

Performance pay may explain why private schools appeal to parents despite the tuition costs. Many private schools pay staff with bonuses of nearly 10% of base pay in contrast to the few public school examples with about 2% (Podgursky & Springer, 2007). When public schools give bonuses and merit pay, moreover, they are more often for an additional credential such as certification by the National Board for Professional Teaching Standards for which there is only mixed evidence for promoting student achievement.

Only 12% of the nation's school districts use any form of merit pay, and the total averages only about 2% of teachers' base salaries (Ballou & Podgursky, 1997). But nearly 30 state legislatures have created policies that allow or encourage performance-based teacher pay systems (Gonring, Teske, & Jupp, 2007) and for good reasons. Research on districts across the nation indicates a positive relationship between performance pay and student achievement (Figlio & Kenny, 2007). Other evidence shows performance pay contributes to better recruitment and retention of quality teachers, which may also positively influence long-term student performance (Reichardt, 2002).

The National Governor's Association Center for Best Practices released a new report on "pay for contribution," that summarizes new approaches to teacher compensation (Hassel & Hassel, 2007). Seventy percent of voters support pay increases for teachers, and even 80% support pay increases if better teachers are paid more than others. About three quarters support additional pay for teaching in high-poverty schools and also for teaching mathematics and science.

Several trends support the spread of new ways to pay teachers:

- growing recognition that education degrees and teaching experience are nearly unrelated to increased student achievement;

- advances in value-added measurement of teachers' effects upon students' academic performance;
- further empirical evidence on the role of compensation policy as a lever for attracting and retaining better performers and improving performance of all staff; and
- increasing voter support for teacher pay reform and growing gubernatorial leadership in many states in launching new teacher compensation policies based on performance.

Pay Teachers for Contribution

Perhaps the best way to fulfill the expectations generated by these considerations is "pay for contribution," a new term gaining recognition among educational policymakers. It means basing pay on teaching that contributes measurably more to student learning (Hassel & Hassel, 2007). Pay for contribution policies can include pay based on performance, the need for staffing difficult schools, skill shortages, advanced roles such as mentoring other teachers, special skill and knowledge, and advanced degrees in subject matter. Hassel and Hassel's (2007) *Improving Teaching through Pay for Contribution,* written for the National Governors Association Center for Best Practices, describes recent state reforms to change teacher pay. It includes insights on performance pay in general as well as on teaching in hard-to-staff schools and in areas of knowledge and skills shortage, such as mathematics and science.

As Hassel and Hassel point out, research suggests that larger incentive pay opportunities significantly increase the number of higher performing teachers. In the United Kingdom schools, for example, successful teachers received pay differentials 15–22% higher, which correlated with significant student learning gains. To attract U.S. teachers to hard-to-staff schools and subjects such as physics, pay differentials of 20–50% may be required (Hassel & Hassel, 2007).

Recent compilations of cross-industry research indicate that performance pay has a significant positive effect on organizational performance. Research on teacher performance pay in Britain concludes that teachers in schools participating in the performance-pay program increased student learning by half a year more than other teachers, on average, during a 2-year period (Atkinson et al., 2004, cited in Hassel & Hassel, 2007). In the British plan for the most recent year of data, teachers in participating schools could receive performance-based pay up to 22% above non-participating schools' teachers. Pay differentials of less than 5% may not be worth the administrative or political cost, but research in industries indicates that even small percentages may be helpful in retaining high performers through public recognition, though efficacy may be increased roughly proportional to the prospective bonus or raise.

According to Hassel and Hassel (2007), several kinds of performance pay plans obtain the best results and meet more employee preferences: reasonable measures of performance; reward for all important work objectives; frequent feedback on progress; substantial incentives for higher performance; and rewards for both high-average and outstanding performers. Bonuses may offer more capacity for rewarding both individual and team contributions. Policymakers, of course, must weigh issues of fairness, transparency, validity, and breadth of applicability to the design of value-added measurement systems related to teacher-student performance.

Avoid Traditional Pay Policies

As documented above, pervasive pay policies are unsupported by research and public opinion. Traditional state and city pay policies, moreover, are often counterproductive. State and city increases in teacher pay typically result in across-the-board increases for all teachers, regardless of current pay and individual contribution. This policy results in salary "compression"; higher paid teachers gain a smaller relative or percentage gain, which encourages them to leave the teaching system. Empirical research evidence, moreover, does not establish a link between the average base pay levels in traditional teacher pay plans and student learning performance (Hanushek, 1997), and no rigorous research supports the idea that across-the-board pay increases improve student achievement (Hassel & Hassel, 2007).

Moreover, traditional pay policies appear to attract and retain less promising teachers and make the field much less competitive than other professions. On average, teachers in the United States are more likely to score in the bottom quartile rather than the top quartile of verbal ability, which is one proven predictor of teaching performance (Walsh & Tracy, 2004). Of course, the gift of verbal expression in teaching would seem a key to clear explanation and stimulating discussion. Teachers in the top quartile of verbal ability are twice as likely to leave teaching after 5 years as those in the bottom quartile (Walsh & Tracy, 2004), which creates further challenges for maintaining instructional quality.

Higher performing teachers, furthermore, earn little more than less capable teachers, and the pay differential has shrunk dramatically over recent decades. "Between the mid-1960s and 2000, the difference in compensation paid to teachers with the highest and lowest college admissions aptitudes shriveled from 37% to a mere 4%" (Hassel & Hassel, 2007, p. 23). In industry, research surveys show that unrewarded higher performers tend to leave for higher pay and are even more likely to do so if they lack advancement opportunities (Hassel & Hassel, 2007). For the same reasons, better teachers may leave the profession.

Provide Initial and Continuing Professional Education

Barber and Mourshed (2007) found that economically advanced countries whose students scored well on international achievement surveys provided an average of 20 weeks in professional coaching for new teachers and devoted a further 10% of teachers' time to it thereafter. Many international research studies (e.g., Phillips, McNaughton, & MacDonald, 2001; Timperley, Bertanees, & Parr, 2006; Timperley, Wilson, Barrar, & Fung, 2007) report substantial effects on students' reading achievement resulting from professional development in literacy training. English and Bareta (2006) report a huge overall effect. Bishop and colleagues (2005, 2006) found large effects on students' mathematics skills.

Based on the studies, seven parts of teachers' professional development proved important to increase student outcomes (Timperley et al., 2007):

- sufficient and efficiently used time for teacher professional development;
- use of external expertise;
- engagement of teachers in development activities regardless of whether they volunteered or not;
- challenging problem-oriented discourses;
- opportunities to interact as a collective community;
- content consistency with wider policy trends; and
- school leaders' involvement in facilitating the professional learning opportunities in school-based initiatives.

Funding for release time from teaching and use of external experts in teachers' professional development may be desirable but not sufficient for positive student outcomes. School leadership practices that appeared to have positive outcomes include:

- active organization of a supportive environment for professional learning and implementation of new practices in classrooms;
- school leaders learning along with teachers;
- provision of alternative visions and targets for student outcomes and subsequent outcome monitoring; and
- practice of shared leadership among both school leaders and teachers.

Thus, successful professional development appears to have consistent features and requires leadership support. In addition, effective professional development links instructional theory with practical classroom applications and provides motivation and guidance to improve student–teacher relationships. Approximately half the interventions in the core studies reviewed by Timperley and others (2007) used assessment data to target instructional improvement and enhance teacher self-regulation.

Apart from listening to those with expertise, no single type of activity was commonly used by all professional development interventions. No individual activity stood out as more effective than others across studies or within particular categories. Content provided through professional development proved to be more important than the type of activity itself. Stronger academic focus occurred in professional development in areas of writing, mathematics, and science, more so than in reading. Listening to experts, when combined with other content-rich, application-oriented activities demonstrated greater capacity to change practice than other activities.

Employ High-Quality Online Teaching and Teachers

One promising innovation for which performance pay or pay for contribution seems particularly applicable is online distance education. State, district, or commercial organizations might enable well-paid star teachers and program developers to develop outstanding content and presentations, particularly for hard-to-staff subjects, which then can be made widely available and used in schools by less stellar staff including less well paid paraprofessionals that manage classrooms rather than provide scarce subject matter and pedagogical skills. Distance education, particularly online programming, is growing rapidly (Moore & Anderson, 2003). State consortia such as the Southern Regional Education Board (for K–12 schools) and the Western Governors University (for higher education) have successful online courses.

Distinguished universities, including Harvard, Stanford, and the Massachusetts Institute of Technology, make available recorded course lectures and discussions to students and sometimes for alumni and others. Offering online credits and degrees in a variety of subjects, the relatively new University of Phoenix is the largest private American university. Motorola University offers electronics and other courses in 13 countries, and calculates that $1 spent on online courses translates to $30 in productivity gains within 3 years. Other organizations such as Hewlett-Packard and the Federal Bureau of Investigation report large cost savings with online courses.

On average, distance instruction effects on K–12 education are positive relative to conventional face-to-face teaching. Effects range from small to moderate (Moore & Anderson, 2003), and continuing improvements combined with cost savings make the prospects highly attractive. The savings over traditional policies might enable superior teachers to be paid much more generously.

For specific aspects of online learning that make for effectiveness, the *Handbook of Distance Education*, (Moore & Anderson, 2003) and works cited therein offer primary resources. In addition, state departments of education and school districts may benefit from the principles of the North American Council for Online Learning's *National Standards for Quality Online Teaching*, which is based on research evidence: The qualified online teacher:

- meets the professional teaching standards established by a state licensing agency or has academic credentials in the field in which he or she is teaching;
- has the prerequisite technology skills to teach;
- plans, designs, and incorporates strategies to encourage active learning, interaction, participation, and collaboration in the online environment;
- promotes student success through regular feedback, prompt response, and clear expectations;
- models, guides, and encourages legal, ethical, safe, and healthy behavior related to technology use;
- has experienced online learning from the perspective of a student;
- understands and is responsive to students with special needs in the online classroom;
- demonstrates competencies in creating and implementing assessments in online learning environments in ways that assure validity and reliability of instruments;
- develops and delivers assessments, projects, and assignments that meet standards-based learning goals and assesses learning progress by measuring student achievement of learning goals;
- demonstrates competencies in using data and findings from assessments and other data sources to modify instructional methods and content and to guide student learning;
- demonstrates frequent and effective strategies that enable both teacher and students to complete self- and pre-assessments;
- collaborates with colleagues; and
- arranges media and content to help students and teachers transfer knowledge most effectively in the online environment.

These standards seem generally reasonable; they are admirably behavioral in emphasizing performance, and many are similar to principles discussed in previous sections of this book, except partially the first: Traditional licensing is not the mark of a superior teacher, unless it requires deep, assessed knowledge of pedagogy and the subject matter.

Thus, research at the school and district levels is less scientifically rigorous than that at the classroom level. Even so, it suggests the plausible idea that, informed by research and experience, the selection, recruitment, and compensation of the teaching force of a school can be constructive determinants of student achievement. The use of the new media including distance education, moreover, is highly promising.

CHAPTER 7

STATES

From 1994–2010, many states instituted content standards, performance standards, collection methods for longitudinal data, and the use of secure test forms each year. The states strengthened institutional capacity for the design and implementation of large-scale assessment programs. The movement to establish standards and statewide assessments was given great impetus by the federal No Child Left Behind Act of 2001. NCLB made a number of now well-known changes in the state–local school relationship. It required districts and schools to disaggregate test scores by ethnicity, poverty, gender, and disability to try to ensure that various groups receive the education required for them to reach proficiency standards. It also required states to establish the proficiency standards and, for those states that had not already done so, to create statewide examinations to measure student proficiency. In addition, federal guidelines required states to assist local education agencies and their schools in attaining state-determined measures of progress, that is, increased percentages of students attaining proficiency on the state exams.

In spite of the apparent intentions of NCLB and state legislation to improve education by improving accountability through standards and assessments, states' standards were, and generally remain, weak, having improved little during the first decade of the century. While 37 states updated or

Improving Student Learning: Action Principles for Families, Classrooms, Schools, Districts, and States, pages 87–108

revised their standards in at least one subject, the average grade for state standards across all subjects, according to a study sponsored by the Fordham Foundation (Finn, Petrilli, & Julian, 2006), was still a "C-minus." The Fordham Foundation estimated that two thirds of the nation's K–12 students attend schools in states with C– standards or below.

Minimal standards are not the only problem states need to confront in order to reform education. Since 2001, state departments of education have had to recast rather quickly their mission from one of mostly overseeing regulatory compliance into providers of technical assistance and other supports to local education agencies and schools. In terms of improving student outcomes, although some progress has been made, state departments of education still face formidable challenges in assisting districts and schools to improve learning. The necessity of reforming standards to make them more rigorous will only compound the need for states to develop well-articulated, responsive systems of support and to take advantage of alternative means of improving student outcomes.

This chapter, then, addresses reforms that seem most promising in four areas of largely state responsibility for initiating and authorizing:

- establishing higher standards that provide motivation and better outcomes for all students, among other benefits;
- developing statewide systems with the capacity to support higher standards, especially in districts and schools that fail to improve sufficiently under even the current, generally low expectations;
- restructuring failing schools; and
- authorizing charter schools.

Though the research on these reforms is generally not as rigorous as that addressed in other chapters, much of it has sufficient factual basis to suggest specific but provisional recommendations.

Define Rigorous Standards

Prior to the enactment of NCLB, research demonstrated achievement links with rigorous state standards for each grade level leading to clear teaching objectives. From 1992–96, North Carolina and Texas, each with high and explicit standards, made greater achievement gains on the National Assessment of Educational Progress (NAEP) in mathematics and reading than other states (Grissmer & Flanagan, 1998). A research study commissioned by the National Education Goals Panel attributed the significant, sustained performance gains to the high standards and the intensity and stability of leadership from the business community and political sector. On the other hand, increased real per-pupil spending, reduced pupil-teacher ratios, and having more teachers with advanced degrees or highly experienced teachers were found to have no effect on achievement gains (Grissmer & Flanagan, 1998, 2001). Key features of education reform efforts in North Carolina and Texas included:

- grade-by-grade standards with aligned curricula and textbooks;
- expectations that all students would meet the standards;
- statewide assessments linked to the standards;
- accountability for results with rewards and sanctions for performance;
- deregulation and increased flexibility in ways the standards can be met; and
- computerized feedback systems for continuous learning improvement.

Hold Schools Accountable for Meeting Standards

The Thomas B. Fordham Foundation's *The State of State Standards 2000* (Braden et al., 2000) defined quality standards and accountability. Good standards are rigorous, clear, written in plain English, able to communicate what is expected of students, and measurable. Good accountability systems are aligned with the standards and include report cards, school ratings, rewards for successful schools, authority to reconstitute failing schools (for example, by replacing the staff), and the actual exercise of such legislated consequences (Braden et al., 2000, Table G-1).

In an updated *The State of State Standards* (Finn et al., 2006), only three states attained nearly perfect grades: California, Indiana, and Massachusetts. Their common hallmarks were visionary leadership, dedication to fighting and winning curriculum battles among educational constituencies, and achieving bipartisan support for the process and end results. The report furthermore finds a link between such strong state standards and gains on the National Assessment of Educational Progress.

Though most states improved little relative to the earlier *State of State Standards* report, Indiana, New York, Georgia, and New Mexico made substantial progress while Utah, Nebraska, New Hampshire, and Wisconsin actually worsened. Four apparent reasons for poor state standards were diffuse, convoluted, committee-based development; lack of consultation with highly skilled content experts; too much reliance on standards developed by educational professional associations; and failure to benchmark or follow examples of successful states.

Education Week's "Quality Counts 2008" reported an average standards grade of B. Indiana, Louisiana, New York, Ohio, South Carolina, Virginia, and West Virginia earned an A. Ten states earned an A-minus. *Education Week* also graded teaching improvement, chance for success, transitions and alignment, school finance, and arguably the most important category, achievement in K–12 schools. The average grade for the United States was a C overall, but the average state earned a D-plus on public school achievement.

Education Week evaluated how well a state's students perform compared with those in the top-ranked state on 18 separate indicators. The index takes into account current state performance, improvements over time, and poverty-based achievement gaps. Massachusetts again led the nation, earning 82.5 points and a B. Maryland was the only other state to receive a B, while New Jersey earned a B-minus. In many of the higher achieving states, achievement gaps remain for children in poverty. Even though states on average attain poor grades for their standards, state assessments often inflate reports of student academic proficiency, especially in reading and in earlier grades (Cronin, Dahlin, Adkins, & Kingsbury, 2007).

Administer Rigorous, External Examinations

In a key study, John Bishop (1996) shows achievement benefits when schools use external, curriculum-based examinations, and policymakers closely monitor the results. Bishop's research analyzes surveys of the examination effects on learning of the nationwide Advanced Placement Program, the New York State Regents Examination, and U.S. state and Canadian provincial assessment systems. Bishop also compares student achievement in the U.S. with that in Asian and European nations. The examinations Bishop studied share two common elements: They are externally and independently developed and monitored, and they test agreed-upon subject matter, which students are to learn within a nation, state, or province. Often given at the end of related courses, they have substantial positive effects on learning (Bishop, 1996). Made publicly available, the examinations and the results allow citizens, policymakers, educators, parents, and students to assess and compare achievement standings and progress.

The largest and most sophisticated international comparative analysis of national achievement yet conducted corroborates Bishop's findings (Woessmann, 2001). Using data from 39 countries that participated in the Third International Mathematics and Science Study, this study found that the highest achieving nations utilize rigorous, external, curriculum-based examinations and closely monitor the results. High achieving nations also provide teachers with considerable discretion over instructional methods.

The substantial effects of large-scale, external examinations appear to result from students' effective preparation in the uniform subject matter in areas of humanities, science, mathematics, and other content areas. Even though each examination varies in its design, such examinations quantify the degree to which standards have been attained by students and schools.

Educators, other than the students' own teachers, grade these exams. So, students have little incentive to challenge their teachers about course content and standards. Students and teachers can then work together more effectively toward the common goal of meeting examination standards. With uniform standards and curricula, teachers concentrate upon how to teach rather than what to teach. In such a system, teachers can also more reliably depend on what students have been taught in prior grades.

Surveys show that the public strongly supports objective testing, higher standards, and greater specificity about what students should learn (Ravitch, 2001). Surveys of students, citizens, and employers, moreover, reveal substantial dissatisfaction with American schools. According to public opinion research sponsored by the Education Testing Service (2005), Americans do not believe that U.S. schools provide a rigorous high school experience for most students. Fewer than one in ten (9%) adults agree that schools set high expectations and significantly challenge most high school students (Education Testing Service, 2005). Non-profit Achieve corroborated these results with a survey in which only 24% of recent high school graduates say that they faced high expectations and were significantly challenged (Hart Research Associates & Public Opinion Strategies, 2005).

Examinations are not only effective but cost-efficient and represent only a miniscule percentage of K–12 expenditures (Hoxby, 2002). Only $234 million went to commercial firms for standardized testing, standard setting, and accountability in the year 2000. This figure was less than a 0.1% of K–12 school costs at the time and amounted to $5.81 per American student. For the 25 states with available information, the total costs per student run between $1.79 and $34.02. States and school districts have paid steadily and substantially more for things that have no such record of effectiveness and cost effectiveness. Class size reduction, for example, has no such record of achievement results. Examination costs, moreover, will undoubtedly decline in the long run because state education agencies estimated the amounts in the midst of states' development of accountability systems. After development and initial revision, much of the accountability data gathering, reporting, and analysis can be routinized at much lower costs.

Another benefit of external examinations is student incentive effects, discussed in Chapter 4. Accurate information on college applicants allows colleges to provide merit scholarships and advanced students to graduate early. In the 1950s, President Robert M. Hutchins of the University of Chicago designed a program to provide early admission to qualified high school students that allowed them to graduate as young as age 18. Many went on for graduate and professional degrees. The results of less substantial but carefully evaluated recent programs show that qualified students allowed to skip to advanced courses learned far more than others who were similarly qualified. Enacted again, "Hutchins degree" programs would save able students' time and allow them longer careers. Families and taxpayers would save money.

Grades, however, cannot provide the accurate, objective information required for all these purposes. Teachers vary enormously in what content they teach, the rigor of their examinations, and in their grading policies. About 80% of the questions on high school teachers' tests concern factual information rather than analysis, synthesis, and evaluation of ideas. The ranking of students within their grade level is little better since the rankings are based on averages of grades.

Some high school students can pass examinations for advanced college work in ancient history, calculus, and physics. Some college seniors cannot pass freshman high school examinations. A major reason for such anomalies is the lack of standards. Schools in the U.S. award diplomas and degrees for seat time, not proficiency. Japan and most advanced Western countries employ examinations that at least partially overcome these comparability problems. Though there are variations in their design, the examinations in the arts, languages, and sciences, for example, are developed in courses and then offered in an entire nation, province, or state. Though the scope of each examination is well known, they are often graded or checked by educators other than the students' own teachers.

Increased accountability has produced some beneficial effects on the content of what students study. According to *The Condition of Education 2007* report (U.S. Department of Education National, Center for Education Statistics, 2007), high school students in the United States are taking more courses in mathematics and science, as well as social studies, the arts, and foreign languages. Since the early 1980s, increases in the number of academic credits earned by students are partly the result of them taking more advanced courses. The average number of credits earned by high school graduates increased from 21.7 credits in 1982 to 25.8 in 2004. Between 1997 and 2005, moreover, the number of students taking Advanced Placement (AP) examinations more than doubled to about 1.2 million, with the numbers of Blacks and Hispanics taking the AP tests growing faster than those for other racial/ethnic groups. *The Condition of Education* shows that college enrollment immediately after high school increased from 49% in 1972 to 69% in 2005 (U. S. Department of Education National, Center for Education Statistics, 2007).

Require Achievement Accountability

Consistent evidence suggests that accountability and incentives work to improve student achievement. Higher achievement in high school, for example, increases the probability of admission to college. During the past 15 years, the payoff for college attendance more than doubled. Higher achievers are also more often admitted into potentially lucrative majors such as engineering and pre-medicine. Higher achieving high school students also tend to graduate from college and enter graduate and professional programs (Bishop, 1996).

As measured on objective examinations, achievement in rigorous high school courses tends to be rewarded in better pay for graduates. As Bishop (1996) points out, employers have substantially increased the premium paid for graduates with higher mathematics achievement. Front-line workers increasingly assume responsibility for functions formerly carried out by engineers and managers, thus requiring higher levels of performance.

Higher academic achievement has positive effects for social, economic, and political conditions in communities. Parents and communities may derive honor and prestige from high achieving youth. High achievers contribute more to their state and local economies, pay more taxes, and, as informed voters and citizens, may raise the quality of civic and community life.

Achievement information yielded by better accountability systems would be valuable to employers making hiring decisions. To the extent that employers pay more to higher achievers, they make their workforce more efficient and increase student incentives to improve. Accurate information would help eliminate subjective racial, sexual, and other biases and the inconsistencies of interviews.

Economically and socially, reading proficiency continues to significantly affect students long after they finish school. Bormuth (1978) surveyed approximately 5,000 people over age 16. He found that, of those employed, 87% reported reading as part of their work responsibilities. The study concluded that workers, on average, spent 141 minutes per day reading—more than a quarter of their workday. That means that on the job reading earned U.S. workers $253 billion, arguably more than they earned for any other activity. Today, with more workers at higher hourly rates possibly reading more, the annual amount paid for reading must be substantially higher.

STATE-LEVEL SUPPORT SYSTEMS

State education agencies (SEAs) increasingly find it difficult to provide sufficient programming to serve the rising numbers of failing schools and will continue to face challenges if the call for more rigorous standards is met.[1] The Center on Education Policy (CEP) surveyed SEA officials in all 50 states and reported that they lack funding and staff to effectively design, implement, monitor, and sustain a high-quality system of support. A SEA

---

[1] This section primarily summarizes key points of Rhim, Hassel, and Redding (2007), "State Role in Supporting School Improvement." Other sources cited in this section are the sources from which Rhim and others construct their research synthesis and are also cited there.

capacity constraint is that federal funding goes directly to local school districts, rather than to SEAs to implement fully functioning statewide systems of support (CEP, 2007). Even so, there are options for SEAs to consider in providing cost-effective services.

The Center on Innovation & Improvement produced the *Handbook on Statewide Systems of Support* (Redding & Walberg, 2007). The *Handbook* offers descriptions of technical assistance, policies, and practices in several exemplary states, which can be useful to creating and implementing state-district partnerships. In their chapter in the *Handbook*, Rhim, Hassel, and Redding (2007) summarize the emergent literature on state systems of support for failing schools and provide a framework for an effective support system. This section summarizes some key research-based recommendations from their chapter in *Handbook on Statewide Systems of Support*. The other chapters in the book may also be useful. Written by state department officials and staff of regional comprehensive centers, the other chapters describe how states have implemented cost-effective system support recommendations.[2]

Provide State-Level Incentives

Perhaps the most pervasive incentive to improve school performance is the public disclosure of school achievement results. Good results can please citizens; poor results signal not only to school administrators and teachers but also to parents and citizens that greater efforts are needed. Furthermore, setting high standards for student proficiency, as discussed previously, can encourage school personnel to exert greater effort and to better align their efforts with state standards.

Federal policy since 2001, of course, offers states stronger incentives than mere disclosure of results. Rhim and others (2007) cite DiBiase's 2005 study illustrating such variations in state interventions. Some states, for example, actively involved themselves in district decision making, including participating in the development and modification of reform plans and monitoring district progress.

States also provide positive incentives for schools taking desired actions to improve performance and achieving certain results, of which funding is the most prominent example. Rhim and others (2007) summarize several research-based examples of financial incentives used by states, including inducements for high-caliber talent to enter teaching, for current effective teachers or promising teaching candidates to teach in difficult-to-staff

---

[2]In addition, the last 55 pages of the *Handbook* are comprised of "Tools to Strengthen Statewide Systems of Support" to "enable an SEA team to self-assess its system of support and plan for its improvement" (p. 271). The book is available for free download at http://www.centerii.org/survey/

schools or high-demand subject areas, for talented school leaders to lead a turnaround effort in a low-achieving school, and for high-performing teachers demonstrating strong achievement results. Other non-financial incentives include greater autonomy in schools to achieve desired results or special recognition.

Build State Capacity to Support Local Educators

In state departments of education, systemic capacity building includes the creation and dissemination of knowledge and the development of effective data systems. Local capacity building involves the direct support and technical assistance provided by states and contracted providers to specific districts and schools. Among the states are several that stand out and are worth studying. Michigan provides MI-MAP online "curriculum for school improvement." Maine, New Hampshire, Rhode Island, and Vermont created a common statewide assessment system, the New England Common Assessment Program (NECAP), aligned with shared grade-level expectations.

States can also help districts improve the supply, quality, and training of teachers (as discussed in Chapter 6) and school leaders through several initiatives, including better credentialing standards and tests to ensure teachers share an established base of knowledge. Legislation may be required to provide teachers with monetary incentives and loan forgiveness programs to work in difficult-to-staff schools. Alternative certification programs may entice mid-career professionals to teach in high-demand subjects. Recognizing the critical role of the principal, some state programs offer principal leadership academies and bonus pay for principals leading successful improvements in student achievement.

Systematic and strategic use of student assessment data about school performance can positively influence student learning (Palaich, Griffin, & van der Ploeg, 2004). Many individual districts and schools do not have the capacity to develop or maintain sufficient data management and interpretation systems on their own and must rely on state-provided data. State data systems vary considerably in efficiency, timeliness, and utility for school improvement purposes. States are now experimenting with data systems that permit longitudinal tracking of student outcomes to measure value-added growth produced by individual teachers, as in Tennessee.

Westat's review of all 50 states' systems of support shows a high degree of heterogeneity in the organizational structures employed to deliver technical assistance to low-achieving schools (Westat, 2006). For example, 32 states provide ongoing assistance regularly to individual schools, though not all onsite; 17 states provide coaching and facilitation to groups of schools and whole districts (Archer, 2006). Archer counts 14 states who report in their consolidated plans that they use intermediate agencies to provide direct support to schools and districts. Nineteen states reported they used external consultants or partners to deliver technical assistance in Fall 2006 consolidated state plans (Archer, 2006). Other states, such as California, do not manage contracts with external providers directly, but offer funds to the individual schools to hire a provider. Research on this approach, however, showed that only 20% of the first cohort of schools that volunteered to receive intervention support met the state's performance growth expectations (Mazzeo & Berman, 2003).

Recruit Distinguished Educators

Several states recruit educators with excellent records of success to serve as improvement facilitators and coaches, and research on some state systems indicates positive results. The Kentucky Distinguished Educator program, for example, established in 1994, shows that the rate of improvement in schools using distinguished educators exceeded the statewide rate of improvement in student performance (David, Kannapel, & McDiarmid, 2000). "After two years, 34 of the first cohort of 53 schools met or exceeded their performance goals. In the second cohort, 167 of 188 schools improved, and 85 of these schools exceeded their goals" (Rhim et al., 2007, p. 42, citing David et al., 2000). Improved achievement was more likely when distinguished educators held full-time positions at the school, were well matched with the school's needs, and stayed at the school for two years (David et al., 2000). Those with extensive experience can mentor future distinguished cohorts.

The available evidence indicates that "regular communication, sharing of information across units unaccustomed to collaborating, and regular reporting of data are central to creating an effective system of support" (Rhim et al., 2007, p. 43). State education agencies can help districts and schools identify their specific technical assistance needs. Some states provide technical assistance directly to schools as the primary point of intervention, others through school districts as the targeted lever of change, and still others work with both schools and districts to coordinate intervention. It does not yet seem clear which alternative works best.

These programs, of course, are not always successful. In South Carolina, for example, only 26 of 73 schools targeted for improvement met their achievement goals (Mazzeo & Berman, 2003). In Maryland, New York, and California, fewer than 20% of the schools receiving state assistance met their performance goals after a year (Reville, 2004).

Provide Targeted State Assistance

According to Rhim and others (2007), state systems of support include the following main services:

- development of improvement plans;
- technical assistance related to curriculum and instruction;
- data training and support for using assessments;
- leadership development; and
- support for parent and community involvement.

The most common service provided is improvement planning. All except three states provide guidance on plan development through means such as visits from outside evaluators (29 states), outside reviews based on documentation (13 states), and self-reviews (17 states) (Archer, 2006). "In addition to planning, 17 states provide leadership training, 15 states provide data analysis training, and 19 states provide special content in professional development" (Rhim et al., 2007, p. 47, citing Archer, 2006).

Monitor State Progress

Though some states have created relatively sophisticated means to assess schools, the metrics for evaluating state systems of support are not as well developed. As discussed throughout this summary of Rhim and others (2007), states vary considerably in the range of services, incentives, consequences, and opportunities provided to low-achieving schools and in the data they gather to study the effectiveness of these interventions and policies. State education agencies often do not have sufficient capacity to assess the costs and benefits of their support systems (Reville, 2004). In order to strengthen states' evaluation systems, Rhim and others (2007, p. 53) cite nine strategies, here slightly reworded, that appear useful:

- tracking sanctions and utilization of incentives;
- tracking resources dedicated to research and development;
- monitoring implementation of new instructional technologies promoted by the state and determining the impact of new practices;
- documenting participation in teacher and leadership training programs and assessing value-added performance in student achievement;
- monitoring schools receiving state support and tracking annual improvement goals;
- monitoring effectiveness of services and changes resulting from service delivery;

- monitoring changes to operations of school districts and schools within districts; and
- tracking opportunities for improved performance created by the state and evaluating impact.

To this list might be added using transformational school-level leadership and external technical assistance for successful school turnaround efforts.

CHARTER SCHOOLS

As documented in previous sections, gradual improvements and even radical restructuring may not lead to substantial achievement progress. For this reason, choice, particularly in the form of charter schools, has expanded dramatically in recent years. As described by Rhim and others (2007), competition for students in a more privatized education market is another incentive for better performance in traditional public schools.

In recent decades, 40 states and the District of Columbia created charter school legislation; 43 states provided interdistrict transfers; and 12 states allowed publicly funded vouchers for students to attend private schools, or tax credits or deductions for private school tuition, or both (Education Commission of the States, 2007; McNeil, 2007). Federal statutes require that states and districts provide public school choice to students in schools that fail to make progress for two years; however, relatively few parents take advantage of this option. Parents may be hampered by late, opaque notification of their rights.

Parents can exercise greater choice and influence in charter schools, which receive government funding and supervision, but are managed by private school boards (Walberg, 2007b). Charter boards may hire their own staff or hire non-profit or for-profit management organizations. State laws vary regarding charter school regulations, and charters must adhere to the terms of their contract with their "authorizer," which is often the local school district, state, or state-appointed charter issuer. Charter schools must then demonstrate acceptable student achievement and sufficient enrollment to stay open.

Charter schools operate somewhat independently of districts and are subject to fewer regulations. Their contract or charter requires them to achieve performance objectives in a defined, multi-year term, usually 5 years. Districts also experiment with new school creation to address historic trends of low achievement in some schools. The Chicago Public Schools, for example, launched Renaissance 2010 which is creating 100 new schools through chartering, performance contracts, and staff replacement to be completed by the end of 2010.

Districts may charter schools, but in 12 states, the state board of education, the state commissioner, or the state department of education may directly authorize charter schools. Other states operate indirectly by hearing appeals of local district denials of charter applications. Once new charter schools are created, states also provide oversight, accountability, and technical assistance, as they would for traditional public schools.

Massachusetts developed a somewhat similar model in its Commonwealth Pilot Schools. Through a partnership agreement with the school district and teachers' union, pilot schools receive substantial autonomy over their budget, staffing, governance, curriculum, assessment, and school calendar. Like charter schools, pilot schools are created to foster innovation and provide research and development sites. To achieve their goals, they can negotiate exemption from district rules and regulations. Unlike most charter schools, teachers in pilot schools are union members. Research by the Center for Collaborative Education (2006) on the Boston Pilot Schools reported that Pilot School students perform better than district averages across every indicator of student engagement and performance, including the state standardized assessments.

Foster Charter Schools

Because of the large and growing number of charter schools, investigators have carried out local, state, and national evaluations, some of which were randomized field trials, and their progress could be compared. Several comprehensive reviews of charter school research (summarized by Walberg, 2007a) show that, on average, charter schools achieve more than comparable traditional public schools. Many parents would prefer to send their children to charter schools but are turned away because states and school districts place caps on the number of charter schools and the number of students that can be enrolled in them.

Follow Evidenced-Based Charter Policies and Practices

Because not all charter schools are successful, Lance Izumi (2008) investigated the charter school policies that appear to promote success. Nearly all these policies are identical or similar to those recommended in other parts of this book, including the use of standards-based curricula and instruction, more study time, knowledgeable teachers, empirically proven teaching methods, and detailed diagnostic analysis of test results.

Rigorous evidence from New York City has now become available on the comparative effectiveness of charter schools and the factors that make charter schools effective in raising achievement. Hoxby, Murarka, and Kang (2009) found that 94% of students in charter schools in the city were admitted by lottery since far more students applied than the number of seats available. This allowed a randomized experiment to compare the achievement progress of students who had been lotteried in with those lotteried out of 43 charter schools. They found that an average minority student from a poor family attending a charter school for eight years would gain enough in mathematics achievement to nearly eliminate the "Harlem-Scarsdale gap" (Harlem being an economically depressed part of the city and Scarsdale being a wealthy suburb). In the same period, two thirds of the reading gap would be reduced.

Charter schools differed from traditional public schools in having a greater number of days in the school year, and a greater number of hours in the school day, as well as practicing direct instruction more often, conducting regular evaluations of student progress, and requiring student uniforms and parent contracts. Distinguishing the more successful charter schools from other charter schools were:

- more days in the school year;
- more hours in the school day;
- more minutes each day devoted to language arts;
- greater use of direct instruction;
- a core knowledge curriculum;
- regular student evaluations;
- parent contracts to support their children's progress;
- teacher pay for performance;
- a school mission statement emphasizing academic performance; and
- the administration of rewards and punishments to establish and maintain student discipline.

Divide Business Management and Educational Leadership

One policy that appears particularly or even uniquely applicable for charter schools is the separation of leadership roles (Izumi, 2008). Outstanding charter school leaders are unlikely to have expertise and skills in real estate acquisition, building management, purchasing, contracting, and other business management functions. School districts, moreover, usually provide such functions for traditional schools but not for charter schools, which, by definition, are more independent and autonomous. Therefore, successful charter schools appear to require not only educational leadership, but also skilled business management.

RESTRUCTURING FAILING SCHOOLS

Students, parents, and teachers are perhaps the most powerful and direct influences on learning. Even so, schools, districts, states, and the federal government are exerting ever-greater indirect influence in response to the general recognition of the need for substantial improvements in achievement. Federal and state legislation are imposing radical reforms.

NCLB requires schools that do not make Adequate Yearly Progress (AYP) for five consecutive years to develop "restructuring" plans. In 2004–05, 22,093 schools missed AYP; and in most cases, they failed to meet achievement targets for "all students" achievement in reading, mathematics, or both (U.S. Department of Education, National Center for Education Statistics, 2007). According to NCLB (§1116(b)(8)(B)(i–v)), schools that miss AYP for 5 years have the following options:

- reopen as a charter school;
- replace "all or most of the school staff (which may include the principal)" most relevant to the failure of the school to make AYP;
- contract with an external management organization "with a demonstrated record of effectiveness";
- turn the "operation of the school over to the State educational agency, if permitted under State law and agreed to by the State"; or
- engage in other "fundamental reforms, such as significant changes in the school's staffing and governance."

According to non-regulatory guidance issued by the U.S. Department of Education (2006), the last option may also include changing governance of the school to increase oversight by the local district, closing and reopening the school with a new focus or theme, reconstituting the school into smaller learning communities, dissolving the school and assigning students to other schools in the district, pairing the restructuring school with a higher performing school, or expanding or narrowing the grades served.

In 2005–06, approximately 600 schools implemented restructuring plans. The Center on Education Policy (2006) forecasted that nearly 2,000 schools were being restructured in 2007–08 and 3,200 in 2008–09. The American Institutes for Research reports that most schools choose (somewhat vague) "Option 5," an alternative form of restructuring (LeFloch, Taylor, & Zhang, 2006). In Michigan, nearly all schools in restructuring (93%) chose Option 5 in 2004–05 (Scott, Kober, Rentner, & Jennings, 2006). About three fourths (76%) of restructuring schools in California used Option 5 in 2005–06 (Scott et al., 2006).

Among the interventions pursued, 42% hired an outside expert to advise the restructuring school, 24% extended the school day or year, and 14% "restructured the internal organization of the school" (Center on Education Policy, 2006). In rare cases, districts hired private firms or asked state education agencies to takeover restructuring schools or reopened them as public charter schools. When restructuring schools chose a more drastic measure, they replaced staff members with more qualified individuals. Fourteen percent of all restructuring schools replaced some or all staff members in 2004–05 (Center on Education Policy, 2006).

Turn Failing Schools Around

In *School Turnarounds: A Review of the Cross-Sector Evidence on Dramatic Organizational Improvement,* Public Impact (2007) reviewed research related to the transformation of low-achieving schools and other organizations from both public and private sectors. The review augments the limited research on school turnarounds with the substantial body of cross-sector research about effective turnaround strategies and turnaround leaders in the public (non-education), non-profit, and business sectors. *School Turnarounds* reviewed 59 documents, mostly case studies (50), to inform the development of an analytical framework for school turnarounds. The review suggests environmental factors that influence prospects for successful turnaround, including timelines for transformation, freedom to act, support and aligned systems, performance monitoring, and community engagement. Public Impact also summarized effective leader actions for turnarounds. Leader actions fall into one of three categories:

- analysis and problem solving,
- driving results, and
- measuring and reporting.

Two specific actions frequently and centrally emerge: concentrating on achieving a few, tangible wins in Year 1 and implementing strategies even when they require deviation from current organizational policies.

The What Works Clearinghouse (WWC) also reviewed research on school turnarounds, which have potential to produce sustainable results and to improve student academic outcomes, student persistence, and student behavior in chronically low-achieving schools. Among the six practice areas in the WWC review (Herman et al., 2008), two areas reinforce the use of turnaround specialists and external professional development providers for substantial school improvement—cultivating and utilizing turnaround specialists and maximizing external support resources.

One of the national resources to support school restructuring and other means of improving low-achieving schools is the Center on Innovation & Improvement (CII) funded by the U.S. Department of Education. It is one of five national content centers that provide technical assistance and guidance to 16 regional comprehensive centers across the country. Working with CII, leading experts on restructuring wrote the *Handbook on Restructuring and Substantial School Improvement* (Walberg, 2007a) to guide regional comprehensive centers to assist states, districts, and schools in establishing policies to restructure schools. The *Handbook* provides information, principles, and tools for restructuring and substantially improving schools.

The *Handbook* presents state-guided plans for systemic district improvement and district principles, defining restructuring as "urgent and substantial improvement including changes in governance." It concentrates on the implementation and monitoring of the restructuring plan, including measuring impact on classroom teaching and learning and continued engagement of stakeholders, particularly the district's board and administration. The restructuring principles form a continuum of increasingly dramatic interventions, which might be avoided by effectiveness at the earlier stages. Complementing the *Handbook* is a set of modules for implementing its principles. Key principles from the modules are:

- District-led reform initiatives should include governance and management reform, data-driven decision making, alignment of incentives and sanctions, and consumer-oriented services.
- A systemic and coherent district-wide initiative, focused on instruction and supported by strong district leadership, can substantially impact the pace and extent of improvement in student achievement.
- Data, evidence-based practices, and knowledge of the change process should be employed when selecting restructuring interventions.
- Effective leadership in a turnaround effort requires developing a mission and goals, managing the educational production function (process), promoting an academic learning climate, and developing a supportive work environment.
- To increase student achievement, use state standards to guide instruction and assessment, employ assessment to evaluate students' progress, and organize instruction selectively to bring all students to proficiency.
- Develop and maintain efficient systems of support that enable individuals in the school community to competently fulfill their roles and achieve clear goals, especially improved student learning.

What is the evidentiary basis of these principles? As pointed out in Chapter 1 and as emphasized by the U.S. Department of Education's Institute of Education Sciences, education policy and practice should be based on evidence derived from well-conceived, well-executed randomized field trials. The next best evidence is that from quasi-experiments and large-scale longitudinal studies, preferably following the progress of individual students.

Since a large portion of educational research falls short of these standards, the modules in the *Handbook* rely on "promising practices" research.

The modules in the *Handbook* synthesize findings from the most rigorous, available research in other fields, including business firms and branches of government, many of which are statistically controlled, correlational studies or analyses of long, outstanding records of improved performance. The *Handbook* authors are experienced educators and experts in their fields commissioned to judiciously weigh the less than definitive evidence and to state guiding principles.

The *Handbook* section on success indicators provides checklists of specific actions for developing and implementing a successful restructuring plan. The section includes checklists that can be used for classroom observation and teacher interviews to assess instructional progress in restructuring schools. Evidence collected with the indicators can be used to identify needs and strengths of the restructuring process and the likelihood of substantial achievement progress.

Three major lessons that emerged from this early review are:

- Low-performing schools achieve large, fast improvements by different methods, not the usual incremental changes over time.
- Radical transformation of academic achievement from low performance is not a one-time project; it is fundamental to the everyday work in schools and districts.
- To be successful in eliminating low performance, schools and districts must have an iron will set firmly on children's learning and achievement.

Though not rigorous, other research suggests several other practices that may be helpful in restructuring schools.

Build Alliances

Research in education and in business often shows that leaders must build alliances and means of communication that push reform forward. Backlash may come from parents, community, interest groups, or others unwilling to embrace change. With an unfaltering commitment and focus on changes that improve student learning, leaders and followers bring about the desired transformation in achievement. Effective, careful governance that includes input from school, district, parents, community leaders, and state levels significantly supports the restructuring process. Managing stakeholders' input, energy, and work effort is positively related to both fresh starts with new staff and other types of turnarounds.

Persist Through Difficulty

Persistence even in the face of repeated failure is another hallmark of successful restructuring. In some cases, the same organizations must undergo repeated restructuring to achieve the desired success. According to one study of Fortune 100 companies, for example, only 30% of restructuring efforts resulted in worthwhile improvements (Pascale, Millemann, & Gioja, 1997). Investment predictions in the business world are that approximately 20% of start-up organizations fail, another 60% show mediocre performance, and only 20% are very successful (Christensen & Raynor, 2003).

Cross-industry surveys of top managers reveal that frequent restructuring is expected in highly competitive, achievement-oriented industries (Kanter, 1991). Failing schools may face similar competition and justifiable expectation among school districts seeking to transform low-achieving schools. Thus, states and districts may expect to restructure failing schools repeatedly until they achieve success.

Consider Local Educators' Recommendations

What do district staff find to be the most effective restructuring principles? From a national survey, the Center on Education Policy (2007) reported the following:

- increasing the use of student achievement data to inform instruction and other decisions (97% used this strategy);
- increasing the quality and/or quantity of teacher and principal professional development (94%); and
- improving the school planning process (93%).

RADICAL RESTRUCTURING

In the last half of the 20th century, American public school teachers were rarely fired for poor achievement, and schools were rarely closed for failure to improve achievement. But NCLB requires states, districts, and schools to more frequently face these challenges. The Center on Innovation & Improvement published three booklets on these topics (Brinson & Rhim, 2009; Kowal, Rosch, Hassel, & Hassel, 2009; Steiner, 2009), which are briefly discussed here.

Break Poor Performance Habits

Brinson and Rhim (2009) cited research that suggests that at least some repeatedly failing schools can improve for two years in a row and carried out case studies of the changes made in five such successful schools. As the authors note, the limited number of schools prevents scientific generalizations about the causes, but it is interesting to note that the role of the local school district was intensive in all five cases, the state's role was moderate to intensive in four cases, and three of the principals were replaced. Additional funding was limited in all five cases, and external partners such as visiting educators were involved in three cases. The authors' detailed reporting on the operational changes made may prove useful in selecting change strategies.

Dismiss Underperforming Staff

Educational leaders may need to initiate involuntary dismissals or encourage voluntary resignations. Kowal and others (2009) summarize research on performance-based dismissals outside of education where the experience base is wider and richer to inform public school turnaround leaders. They also specify the ways which school, state, and district leaders may initiate staff replacement.

Kowal and others recommend that school turnaround leaders make their goals and expectations clear, gather and analyze relevant information about individual employees' performance, share the information with dismissal candidates, and seek their reaction. Taken carefully, these steps can justify dismissals.

States and districts can facilitate these steps by empowering leaders to reform tenure protections, seniority rights, and other job protections to enable such dismissals. They can provide turnaround principals with greater autonomy about staffing decisions, give them the first choice of high-quality teacher applications to the district, allow special monetary and non-monetary incentives for teachers that demonstrate superior results, and make available teams of specialists familiar with such principles and the regulations for dismissals.

Close and Reopen Persistently Failing Schools

Also under the sponsorship of the Center on Innovation & Improvement, Steiner (2009) reviewed research literature on school closings, examined media accounts, and carried out structured interviews on closing failing schools. She specifically looked at schools in Denver, Colorado; Hartford, Connecticut; Chicago, Illinois; and Pittsburgh, Pennsylvania. From the information and insights gathered, she recommended the following steps:

- consider school closure in the context of larger district reform efforts;
- use data to guide decision-making at each stage;
- explain to the public how students will benefit;
- avoid contentious battles with school board members;
- provide support to students and families during the transition;
- clarify the new principal's role in the transition; and
- provide staff members with clear information about the steps.

Recruit and Select Systematic Leaders

As pointed out in the *Handbook on Restructuring and Substantial School Improvement* (Walberg, 2007a), successful restructuring often requires substantial changes in the direction and governance of a school. Though the right leader can make a large difference, a single person cannot effectively sustain the transformation. Based on cross-sector evidence on dramatic performance improvement, two paths lead to higher results: substantial changes with largely the same staff or fresh starts with new or mostly new staff. Either may depend on the organization's leader (generally a new person) implementing new practices to transform the organization and its performance substantially and rapidly.

The choice of leader is paramount in restructuring. Effective turnaround leaders combine the qualities of entrepreneurs and traditional organization leaders. They focus persistently on a small number of high-priority goals in order to obtain quick victories that teach the staff how to perform well. Leaders in successful turnarounds engage many people in achieving higher levels of performance. They do not do it all themselves. They utilize the talents and resources of staff, parents, external consultants, and the students.

Even so, since poor school achievement is a national predicament, perhaps the term "strong leadership" is too weak if rigorous research on successful business firms is taken as a guide for choosing educational leaders, especially for turnaround schools but perhaps for all schools and positions of school leadership at all levels. Detailed personality assessments of 316 chief executive officers of business firms showed that successful leaders were no more likely than other CEOs to be good listeners, team builders, colleagues, or communicators (Kaplan, Klebanov, & Sorensen, 2008). The leadership traits that distinguished them were persistence, attention to detail, analytic thoroughness, and the ability to work long hours.

Parallel with school and district policies, the state policies discussed in this chapter can encourage and reinforce if not require effective education. In difficult cases, radical restructuring may be necessary. In addition, some principles, also discussed in this chapter, can be best carried out or supported by states under the present organization of American public education.

CHAPTER 8

CONCLUSION: SCIENCE, WISDOM, AND COMMON SENSE

Today's scientific investigations of school learning seldom acknowledge the early anticipation of modern ideas and findings that can be traced from Greece's Golden Age of Plato and Aristotle through 17th Century English philosophy to early American psychological science emphasizing evidence and pragmatism. It seems reasonable then, in conclusion, to point out how some of the most important themes in the previous chapters accord with much older ideas and the common sense of many of today's parents and teachers as well.

Some Greek philosophers espoused that to learn, children need only reminders of ideas they already know—perhaps even at birth—but Aristotle held that children initially acquire ideas through deliberate teaching and other experience, and that the "association of ideas" constitutes learning. He also emphasized that "we become what we do"; therefore, good habits are essentials of education. (For quotes and detailed explanations of philosophy and historical psychology in this section, see the online *2009 Stanford Encyclopedia of Philosophy*.)

Improving Student Learning: Action Principles for Families, Classrooms, Schools, Districts, and States, pages 109–114

ACQUIRING AND ASSOCIATING IDEAS

About 2000 years after Aristotle, the English philosopher John Locke advanced the hypothesis that people learn primarily from external stimulation. In "An Essay Concerning Human Understanding" (1690), he maintained that at birth the human mind is a "blank slate," empty of ideas. The senses provide simple ideas, and the mind then combines the information provided by the senses into more complex ideas.

Anticipating American pragmatism and common sense of three centuries later, Locke recommended learning that prepares children to manage their social, economic, and political affairs when they become adults. In "Some Thoughts Concerning Education" (1697), he held that a foundational education should begin in early childhood, and that the teaching of reading, writing, and arithmetic should be gradual and cumulative.

Consistent with these philosophical views is *The Application of Psychology to the Science of Education*, by Johann Friedrich Herbart (1898), who is considered one of the founders of scientific methods of education. Effective teaching, he argued, requires identifying the learner's interests and connecting them with what they are to learn.

Inspired by Herbart, the American Herbartian Society specified five steps of teaching the "apperceptive mass" of associated ideas, made famous around 1930:

- Motivate students for the lesson;
- Present the lesson;
- Associate new lesson ideas with those studied earlier;
- Illustrate the lesson's major points with examples; and
- Assess the students for their mastery of the lesson.

Thus, the ideas and recommended practices from ancient philosophy and from the beginnings of scientific psychology are consistent with what is described as the elements of learning and teaching described in the earlier chapters.

SINGLE TASKING

Another idea, seemingly new but clearly anticipated much earlier, deserves emphasis, particularly in our own times. Philosophers and early scientific psychologists urged avoidance of what today appears a great and common danger to both children and adults—"multitasking" or trying to do several things simultaneously. In his often reproduced 1740s letters to his son, Lord Chesterfield advised that undivided attention is the key to learning mastery and even genius, since he argued "hurry, puzzle, and agitation are the never failing symptoms of a weak and frivolous mind."

William James agreed in his classic *Principles of Psychology* (1890), "The faculty of voluntarily bringing back a wandering attention over and over again is the very root of judgment, character, and will." James often spoke to educators and emphasized the same idea in his 1925 collection *Talks to Teachers on Psychology and to Students on Life's Ideals.* The dangers of trying to do several things at once is even more threatening today, particularly in the case of media multitasking in the form of television, internet, video games, text messages, cell phones, and e-mail. In *Managing the Knowledge Workforce*, Jonathan Spira (2009) estimated that multitasking workers' information overload cost the U.S. economy $650 million a year in lost productivity.

With shorter attention spans, children are undoubtedly all the more susceptible to a multiplicity of stimuli at home and at school. Even in their classrooms, other children's restless movements and misbehavior, announcements over the public address system, the prospect of exciting sports after school, and the like can distract attention from teachers explanations, textbooks, and perhaps most important, children's personal reflections about what they are learning, what they have learned in the past, and how the two are associated.

The early chapters of this book explained how parents, teachers, and students themselves can avoid such problems and accomplish these things. To accomplish them, the remaining chapters described how to establish and maintain the most advantageous settings at the classroom, school, school district, and state levels. The careful reader may have noticed that some practices have been found and documented at several of these levels and are therefore repeated as themes in more than one chapter. It can be hoped that the entirety of the research findings will be helpful to all parents, educators, and policymakers intending to help improve the productivity of American schools.

APPENDIX

In basing practice on rigorous scientific research, education is following agriculture and medicine by several decades. These pioneering fields have compared the effects of well-estimated alternative practices, evaluated their relative sizes, and educated practitioners—farmers, doctors, and educators—who may best know about the costs and difficulties of implementation. In the case of farmers, the outcome of interest might be yield per acre; in medicine, the diminution of morbidity and mortality; in education, increased rates of learning and school completion.

Since all science is fallible, the synthesis of multiple studies is necessary for a solid foundation of applied science and practice. In the past few decades, education researchers have steadily produced many findings, and the most important findings can now be shared in this book.

Bringing together many hard-won findings, John Hattie (2009) provided estimates of the sizes of the effects estimated in more than 52,000 studies so that they may be readily compared. In his book, he usefully divided the results into separate chapters on the student, home, school, teacher, curricula, and teaching (but not on the additional agents—the district, school, and state—as in this book). Hattie drew on a huge volume of findings under each of his topics. With respect to teaching, for example, he found 365 syntheses of nearly 26,000 studies involving more than 52,000 teachers, students, and others.

To illustrate the comparative sizes of effects, Table 3 below shows a selection of the effects compiled by Hattie. As indicated, the first panel shows the relative sizes of the better-established, causal effects of what is likely to seem to many educators as workable practices. Those selected for reporting in this book and in the first panel have been investigated relatively rigorously in randomized experiments and statistically well-controlled comparative studies. Many are familiar and appear practical to experienced educators.

The second panel shows Hattie's estimates of what appear as causally uncertain, questionable, or unalterable effects of conditions, practices, and programs. Educators, for example, have little control over birth weight, socioeconomic status, and residential moving. Nor can teachers usually control what students have learned before they come to them.

Even in the first panel, moreover, the sizes of some of the effects may be poorly estimated. Homework effects, for example, may be underestimated not because homework has relatively weak effects as reported in the table but because weak students may do homework or more of it while quick students might get by even though skipping it. Similarly, since more able students may be assigned to accelerated programs, the cause of apparent program success may be the students' ability, not the programs themselves. In addition, depending on the degree and quality of implementation of the programs and practices, the effect may vary considerably from the estimates in the table.

Still more tentative are the findings on causally plausible, seemingly effective features of schools, districts, and states discussed in their respective chapters. The research is too limited and insufficiently rigorous to afford numerical estimates of their effects. Thus, education science is far from the beginning of its end, but perhaps is at the end of its beginning.

The research, nonetheless, is worth considering since administrators and policymakers at these levels provide resources and set the stage for classroom teaching and learning. As reported in previous chapters, for example, repeated investigations of the features of unusual cases such as high-poverty schools that achieve well, at the upper third of all schools, may be sufficiently revealing and plausible not only to justify further research but to cautiously suggest promising practices for implementation and evaluation.

Even policies and practices with relatively small effects, moreover, deserve consideration and possible implementation. Roughly speaking, a positive effect of only 10 or 15 points would serve over ten years to accelerate learning of a typical child in poverty to the achievement level of a middle-class student. The combination of multiple practices over years remains to be investigated but is likely to substantially raise learning rates, such that students might achieve in six years what is expected of high school graduates, and high school graduates might achieve as well as today's college graduates.

TABLE 3. Estimates of Effects on Achievement

Major Learning Agent	Better Causally Established, Workable Practices	Effect
Teacher	Provide ongoing monitoring and feedback	75
Teacher	Repeatedly video tape teachers learning a new skill and provide performance feedback till mastered	73
Teacher	Provide accelerated instruction for quick or advanced learners	73
Teacher	Teach using behavioral cues and feedback	65
Teacher	Teach students to teach acquired knowledge and skills to others	59
Teacher	Provide feedback to learners on progress	58
Teacher	Space learning over multiple occasions rather than cramming	56
Teacher	Teach students to set goals to attain and questions to answer	43
Teacher	Avoid "labeling" or stereotyping students as in traditional special education	46
Teacher	Teach word-attack skills to beginning readers	45
Teacher	Teach students study skills	44
Teacher	Directly teach what the curriculum requires	44

(continues)

TABLE 3. Continued

Major Learning Agent	Better Causally Established, Workable Practices	Effect
Teacher	Devote time to teaching reading comprehension	43
Teacher	Use mastery principles to gain "automaticity" of early learning such as letter recognition in reading	43
Teacher	Provide worked examples to build understanding	43
Teacher	State course, unit, and lesson goals	41
Teacher	Use computer-assistant instruction	22
Teacher	Frequent classroom testing	19
Teacher	Homework (effect larger if feedback provided)	14
School	Provide accelerated classes for quick learners	73
Student	Prior learning	52
Home	Prevailing environment for academic learning	42
Home	Socioeconomic status	65
Home	Birth weight	39
Teacher	Classroom climate	37
Home	Peer group outside school	38
Home	Parent involvement in school	36
Teacher	Time spent learning	23
School	Within-class ability grouping of gifted students	15
Teacher	Home visits	14
School	Summer school	8
Teacher	Teaching test taking skills	7

Major Learning Agent	Conditions, Practices, and Programs with Less Rigorous Evidence, Less Alterability, Negative Effects, or a Combination	Effect
School	Extracurricular programs	2
Teacher	"Whole Language" teaching of reading and writing simultaneously	—9
School	Summer vacation	—27
School	Grade retention	—31
Home	Leisure television watching	—33
Home	Residential moving	—49

Note: The size estimates in this table were selected, derived, and recalculated from Appendix B of John Hattie's (2009) book. As explained in the text above, they are classified here, not by Hattie, into the two panels in the table to separate the better-evidenced and workable practices from others that seem less well evidenced and less workable. They were recalculated to make them comparable to conventional effect sizes, and the decimal points are omitted.

CHAPTER 9

APPLICATION OF *IMPROVING STUDENT LEARNING*

Sam Redding

The Academic Development Institute (ADI) and its Center on Innovation & Improvement (CII) follow a tried and proven method for bringing research to practice. First, we define a topic and commission leading researchers to synthesize relevant research and distill from it action principles that can guide the work of educators. Then, we develop tools to assist educators in applying the principles to their particular situations, including plain language, practical indicators of effective practice. Finally, we work alongside the educators to improve the tools, create new tools, and adapt the tools to the myriad contexts within which they operate. *Improving Student Learning* is a needed addition to our library of research syntheses, fleshing out many new domains for consideration and suggesting new tools and refinement of existing ones. Our ultimate goal is to provide educators with a comprehensive and coherent roadmap that connects research to practice and gives procedural guidance to facilitate efficient implementation. For that reason, we choose with care the topics to research and develop, with a view to each topic's significance and place within the overall system of education.

While the educators served by the Academic Development Institute range from state education agencies to school districts, schools, school

Improving Student Learning: Action Principles for Families, Classrooms, Schools, Districts, and States, pages 115–125

leaders, teachers, and family/community facilitators, our goal is always to help those closest to the students make the best decisions for the students—students they know and care about. This requires a ladder of coherent and effective support that begins from the perspective of the student at the top of the ladder and connects each rung of support, as explained in this book and illustrated in the tables below. Each rung in the ladder has its distinct role and responsibilities in order to achieve the desired results for each and every student. Students are best served when each level in the education system meets its responsibilities with high competence, knows the bounds of its authority, and honors and supports the good work of the other levels.

The ultimate goal in a state or district system of support for school improvement is for the people attached to a school to drive its continuous improvement for the sake of their own children and students. When that does not happen, intervention by the state and/or district may be necessary to ensure that students are well served. The result of the intervention, however, must be both improved student performance and changed operational conditions and practice that enable the people closest to the students to sustain and build upon the intervention's successes. All of this requires a coherent and responsive system that includes the state, the district, the school, and organizational partners. Such a system encourages innovation and responsibility at each level.

Finding the right balance of autonomy (freedom to act and innovate), support (information, tools, training, coaching, consultation), and intervention (sanctions and strong direction) among the state, district, school, and classroom is critical in providing conditions conducive to continuous improvement and, for that matter, rapid improvement when current performance is unacceptable. Too heavy a hand from above extinguishes innovation and ownership below. Too little support leaves people of good intention with resources of expertise and information insufficient to the challenges they face. The inability to intervene in situations where students are persistently short-changed is unfair to the students most in need of a high-quality system of education. Without external standards of acceptable performance, and examples of excellence, a state, district, school, or classroom has no gauge to measure its current performance or higher vision on which to set its sights. Again, getting the balance right is critical, and honoring and supporting the good work at each level is essential.

Dr. Walberg has addressed each rung in the education ladder, synthesized the research, and provided us with action principles. For many of these action principles, ADI and CII have provided tools for educators, including various publications, manuals, guides, templates, web-based search engines, and the Indistar® web-based improvement system now used by several states in hundreds of districts and thousands of schools. But Dr. Walberg has given us new ground to break, including subject-specific guidance in literacy, mathematics, science, and teaching additional languages; social-emotional learning; out-of-school activities; pre-school programs; staffing; student and teacher incentives; and charter schools. We have work to do.

The ladder of support for student learning extends from the student at the top rung, through the family, classroom, school, district, and finally to the state as the foundation of the school system. The lower rungs generally support the upper rungs. The resources currently available from the Academic Development Institute and its Center on Innovation & Improvement are listed below in Table 1: Resources, with abbreviations that apply to Table 2. Table 2: The Ladder of Support for Student Learning aligns the action principles included in this book with our resources (see *www.centerii.org* and also Information Age Publishing at *www.infoagepub.com*). These resources provide specific indicators of effective practice related to the action principles, as well as educator guidance. See also the other national content centers for additional resources (links to centers and resources are included in the *Handbook on Effective Implementation of School Improvement Grants*, downloadable from *www.centerii.org*).

Table 1. Resources from the Academic Development Institute and Center on Innovation & Improvement.

Abbreviation	Title or Description
Breaking the Habit	*Breaking the Habit of Low Performance: Successful School Restructuring Stories*
Charter Schools	*Retrofitting Bureaucracy: Factors Influencing Charter Schools' Access to Federal Entitlement Programs*
Coaching	*A Guide for School Improvement Coaches and their Supervisors*
Coherence	*Coherence in Statewide Systems of Support*
Dismissals	*Performance-Based Dismissals: Cross-Sector Lessons for School Turnarounds*
District Pathways	*Exploring the Pathway to Rapid District Improvement*
Evaluating Parent Programs	Redding, S., and Keleher, J. (2010). Evaluating Parent Programs. In *Promising Practices to Support Family Involvement in Schools*, Diana B. Hiatt-Michael, ed. Charlotte, NC: Information Age Publishing.
Evaluating SSOS	*Evaluating the Statewide System of Support*
Idaho Transformation	*Transforming a Statewide System of Support: The Idaho Story*
Indistar®	A web-based tool for district and school improvement made available and supported by the state
Leader Actions	*School Turnarounds: Leader Actions and Results*
Mega System	*The Mega System: Deciding, Learning Connecting; Handbook on Continuous Improvement*
PA System	*Singing Out of the Same Songbook: The Standards-Aligned System in Pennsylvania*
Parent Involvement Analysis	A web-based needs assessment tool for school-level parent involvement with a library of downloadable resources
Restructuring	*Handbook on Restructuring and Substantial School Improvement*
SES Quality	*Improving SES Quality: State Approval, Monitoring, and Evaluation of Supplemental Educational Services*

SIG Handbook	*Handbook on Effective Implementation of School Improvement Grants*
SIG Webinars	A series of pre-recorded, narrated webinars and Power Points on topics related to School Improvement Grants, including the four intervention models. SIG Webinars are produced by the Center on Innovation & Improvement and the Council of Chief State School Officers for the National Network of State School Improvement Leaders.
Solid Foundation®	A school-based, team process, supported by a web tool and resources, to build a strong school community focused on student academic and social learning
SSOS Handbook	*Handbook on Statewide Systems of Support*
Tough Decisions	*Tough Decisions: Closing Persistently Low-Performing Schools*
Transformation Toolkit	Toolkit for the district and school implementation the transformation intervention model
Turnaround Evidence	*School Turnarounds: Cross-Sector Evidence on Dramatic Organizational Improvement*

Most materials below are available for free download from *www.centerii.org*. See Download Publications for full citations. Also, books are available from Information Age Publishing at *www.infoagepub.com*. See also *www.indistar.org*, *www.families-schools.org*, and *www.adi.org*.

TABLE 2. The Ladder of Support for Student Learning

Students: The Top Rung in the Ladder

Action Principles	ADI and CII Resources
Build on Students' Prior Knowledge	Indistar®; *Restructuring, Mega System*
Coordinate Subject Matter Across Grade Levels	Indistar®; *Restructuring, Mega System*
Motivate Students	Indistar®; *Restructuring, Mega System*
Employ Incentives	See Chapter 2 in this book.
Increase Learning Time	Indistar®; *Restructuring, Mega System*
Space Learning Episodes Over Time	Indistar®; *Restructuring, Mega System*
Monitor and Encourage Homework Completion	Indistar®; *Restructuring, Mega System;* Parent Involvement Analysis, Solid Foundation®
Make Use of Summer School	See Chapter 2 in this book.
Encourage Self Instruction	Indistar®; *Restructuring, Mega System*
Foster Academically-Constructive Out-of-School Activities	See Chapter 2 in this book.
Deliver High Quality Instruction	Indistar®; *Restructuring, Mega System*
Foster Classroom and Peer Group Morale	Indistar®; *Restructuring, Mega System*
Encourage Beneficial Peer Groups	
Minimize Unconstructive Time with Mass Media	*Mega System;* Parent Involvement Analysis, Solid Foundation®
Communicate with Parents	Indistar®; *Restructuring, Mega System;* Parent Involvement Analysis, Solid Foundation®

Families: The Student's First Level of Support

Action Principles	ADI and CII Resources
Conduct Effective School Parenting Programs	Indistar®; *Restructuring, Mega System;* Parent Involvement Analysis, Solid Foundation®
Rigorously Evaluate Parent Programs	*Evaluating Parent Programs*
Communicate with Parents	Indistar®; *Restructuring, Mega System;* Parent Involvement Analysis, Solid Foundation®

Classrooms: Where Students, Teachers, and Content Meet

Build on Prior Learning	Indistar®; *Restructuring*; *Mega System*
Align Curriculum and Instruction with Standards	Indistar®; *Restructuring*; *Mega System*
Allocate Learning Time Wisely	Indistar®; *Restructuring*; *Mega System*
Provide High-Quality Instruction	Indistar®; *Restructuring*; *Mega System*
Activate Prior Knowledge	Indistar®; *Restructuring*; *Mega System*
Activate Motivation	Indistar®; *Restructuring*; *Mega System*
Increase Learning Time	Indistar®; *Restructuring*; *Mega System*
Improve Instruction	Indistar®; *Restructuring*; *Mega System*
Increase Classroom Morale	Indistar®; *Restructuring*; *Mega System*
Improve Instruction	Indistar®; *Restructuring*; *Mega System*
Foster Immersion	See Chapter 4 in this book.
Improve Instructional Delivery	Indistar®; *Restructuring*; *Mega System*
Engage Prior Learning	Indistar®; *Restructuring*; *Mega System*
Coordinate Subjects Across Grade Levels	Indistar®; *Restructuring*; *Mega System*
Motivate Students to Learn	Indistar®; *Restructuring*; *Mega System*
Deepen the Learning Experience	Indistar®; *Restructuring*; *Mega System*

Schools: The Context for Classrooms and School Communities

Increase Opportunity to Learn and Class Time	Indistar®; *Restructuring*; *Mega System*
Employ Effective Schools Practices	Indistar®; *Restructuring*; *Mega System*
Align Content to Standards	Indistar®; *Restructuring*; *Mega System*
Provide Challenging, Well-Defined Student Goals	Indistar®; *Restructuring*; *Mega System*
Offer Student Incentives	See Chapter 5 in this book.

(continued)

TABLE 2. Continued

Action Principles	ADI and CII Resources
Increase Learning Time	Indistar®; *Restructuring, Mega System*
Provide Effective Instruction	Indistar®; *Restructuring, Mega System*
Grade Students in Accord with Their Mastery	Indistar®; *Restructuring, Mega System*
Monitor Response to Intervention	
Act on Response to Intervention	
Employ coherent, ambitious instruction	Indistar®; *Restructuring, Mega System*
Build professional capacity	Indistar®; *Restructuring, Mega System*
Strengthen parent-community ties	Indistar®; *Restructuring, Mega System;* Parent Involvement Analysis, Solid Foundation®
Use school leadership as a driver of change	Indistar®; *Restructuring, Mega System; Leader Actions*
Foster a positive learning environment	Indistar®; *Restructuring, Mega System*
Begin Academically-Focused Social and Emotional Learning Programs	See Chapter 5 in this book.
Identify Appropriate Social and Emotional Learning Programs	See Chapter 5 in this book.
Link Social and Emotional Activities to School Programs	See Chapter 5 in this book.
Promote Community Service to Build Empathy	See Chapter 5 in this book.
Build Social and Emotional Skills Systemically and Cumulatively	See Chapter 5 in this book.
Initiate School-Parent Programs	Indistar®; *Restructuring, Mega System;* Parent Involvement Analysis, Solid Foundation®
Plan coherent activities for realizing high standards	Indistar®; *Restructuring, Mega System; Leader Actions*
Engage people and resources to realize high standards	Indistar®; *Restructuring, Mega System; Leader Actions*
Support enabling activities for academic and social learning	Indistar®; *Restructuring, Mega System; Leader Actions*

| Advocate for the needs of students within and beyond the school | Indistar®; *Restructuring; Mega System; Leader Actions* |
| Communicate with staff and community members | Indistar®; *Restructuring; Mega System; Leader Actions;* Parent Involvement Analysis; Solid Foundation® |

Districts: Organization and Support for the Schools

Focus on student achievement and learning	Indistar®; *Restructuring; District Pathways; SIG Handbook; Transformation Toolkit*
Work from a plan of clear goals and improvements	Indistar®; *Restructuring; District Pathways; SIG Handbook; Transformation Toolkit*
Commit to professional learning opportunities	Indistar®; *Restructuring; District Pathways; SIG Handbook; Transformation Toolkit*
Use data to guide improvement	Indistar®; *Restructuring; District Pathways; SIG Handbook; Transformation Toolkit*
Enact comprehensive, coherent reform policies	Indistar®; *Restructuring; District Pathways; SIG Handbook; Transformation Toolkit*
Require educators to accept responsibility for student learning	Indistar®; *Restructuring; District Pathways; SIG Handbook; Transformation Toolkit*
Provide educators with helpful support	Indistar®; *Restructuring; District Pathways; SIG Handbook; Transformation Toolkit*
Monitor programs regularly and intervene if necessary	Indistar®; *Restructuring; District Pathways; SIG Handbook; Transformation Toolkit*
Employ Well-Educated, Knowledgeable Teachers	Indistar®; *Restructuring; District Pathways; SIG Handbook; Transformation Toolkit;*
Employ Valid Screening Tests	
Pay Teachers for Performance	*SIG Handbook; Transformation Toolkit*
Pay Teachers for Contribution	See Chapter 6 in this book.
Avoid Traditional Pay Policies	See Chapter 6 in this book.
Provide Initial and Continuing Professional Education	Indistar®; *Restructuring; District Pathways; SIG Handbook; Transformation Toolkit*
Employ High-quality Online Teaching and Teachers	See Chapter 6 in this book.

(continued)

TABLE 2.   Continued

Action Principles	ADI and CII Resources
States: Coherent Systems of Support for Districts and Schools	
Define Rigorous Standards	*SSOS Handbook; Coherence; Evaluating SSOS; PA System; Idaho Transformation*
Hold Schools Accountable for Meeting Standards	*SSOS Handbook; Coherence; Evaluating SSOS; PA System; Idaho Transformation*
Administer Rigorous, External Examinations	*SSOS Handbook; Coherence; Evaluating SSOS; PA System; Idaho Transformation*
Require Achievement Accountability	
Provide State Level Incentives	Indistar®; *SSOS Handbook; Coherence; Evaluating SSOS; PA System; Idaho Transformation; Coaching*
Build State Capacity to Support Local Educators	Indistar®; *SSOS Handbook; Coherence; Evaluating SSOS; PA System; Idaho Transformation; Coaching*
Recruit Distinguished Educators	Indistar®; *SSOS Handbook; Coherence; Evaluating SSOS; PA System; Idaho Transformation; Coaching*
Provide Targeted State Assistance	Indistar®; *SSOS Handbook; Coherence; Evaluating SSOS; PA System; Idaho Transformation; Coaching*
Monitor State Progress	Indistar®; *SSOS Handbook; Coherence; Evaluating SSOS; PA System; Idaho Transformation; Coaching*
Foster Charter Schools	*SSOS Handbook; Charter Schools*
Follow Evidenced-based Charter Policies and Practices	*SSOS Handbook; Charter Schools*

Divide Business Management and Educational Leadership	See Chapter 7 in this book.
Turn Failing Schools Around	*Indistar®; Restructuring; Turnaround Evidence; Leader Actions; Breaking the Habit; SIG Handbook; Transformation Toolkit; Coaching*
Break Poor Performance Habits	*Breaking the Habit; SIG Webinars; SIG Handbook*
Dismiss Underperforming Staff	*Dismissals; SIG Webinars; SIG Handbook*
Close and Reopen Persistently Failing Schools	*Tough Decisions; SIG Webinars; SIG Handbook*
Recruit and Select Systematic Leaders	*Restructuring; Leader Actions; SIG Handbook; Transformation Toolkit; Coaching; SIG Webinars*

REFERENCES

American Board for Certification of Teacher Excellence. (2007, Spring). *A higher standard.* Washington, DC: Author. Retrieved from http://www.abcte.org/system/files/HigherStandard_Spring07.pdf

Archer, J. (2006, September 13). Building capacity. *Education Week,* S3–S12.

Atkinson, A., Burgess, S., Croxson, B., Gregg, P., Propper, C., Slater, H., & Wilson, D. (2004, December). *Evaluating the impact of performance-related pay for teachers in England* (Working Paper No. 04/113). Bristol, England: Centre for Market and Public Organisations, University of Bristol.

Bakermans-Kranenburg, M. J., van Izendoorn, M. H., & Bradley, R. H. (2005). Those who have, receive: The Matthew effect in early childhood intervention in the home environment. *Review of Educational Research, 75*(1), 1–26.

Ballou, D., & Podgursky, M. (1997). *Teacher pay and teacher quality.* Kalamazoo, MI: W. E. Upjohn Institute.

Barber, M., & Mourshed, M. (2007, September). *How the world's best performing school systems come out on top.* New York: McKinsey. Retrieved from http://www.mckinsey.com/App_Media/Reports/SSO/Worlds_School_Systems_Final.pdf

Barton, P. E., & Coley, R. J. (2007). *The family: America's smallest school—policy information report.* Princeton, NJ: Educational Testing Service.

Bennett, W. J., Finn, C. E., & Cribb, J. T. E. (1999). *The educated child: A parents guide from preschool through eighth grade.* New York, NY: Free Press.

Bergan, J. R. (1977). *Behavioral consultation.* Columbus, OH: Charles E. Merrill.

Bergan, J. R., & Kratochwill, T. R. (1990). *Behavioral consultation and therapy*. New York, NY: Plenum.

Bernard, R. M., Abrami P. C., & Lou, Y. (2004). How does distance education compare with classroom instruction? A meta-analysis of the empirical literature. *Review of Educational Research, 74*(3), 379–439.

Betts, J. R., & Costrell, R. M. (2001). Incentives and equity under standards-based reform. In D. Ravitch (Ed.), *Brookings papers on education policy, 2001* (pp. 9–74). Washington, DC: Brookings Institution.

Bishop, J. H. (1996). The impact of curriculum-based external examinations on school priorities and student learning. *International Journal of Educational Research, 23*(8), 653–752.

Bishop, R., Berryman, M., Cavanaugh, T., & Teddy, L. (2006). *Te Kotahitanga Phase 3 Whanaungatanga: Establishing a culturally responsive pedagogy of relations in mainstream secondary school classrooms*. Report to the Ministry of Education, Wellington, New Zealand.

Bishop, R., Berryman, M., Powell, A., & Teddy, L. (2005). *Te Kotahitanga: Improving the educational achievement of Maori students in mainstream education. Phase 2: Towards a whole school approach* (progress report and planning document). Wellington, New Zealand: Ministry of Education.

Boekaerts, M. (2002). *Motivation to learn*. International Academy of Education Educational Practices Series, H. J. Walberg (Ed.). Geneva, Switzerland: UNESCO, International Bureau of Education. Retrieved from http://www.ibe.unesco.org/en/services/publications/educational-practices.html

Boots, J. (2007). *Student achievement and ABCTE Passport to Teaching Certification in elementary education*. Paper presented at the annual meeting of the American Educational Research Association, Chicago, IL.

Bormuth, J. R. (1978). Value and volume of literacy. *Visible Language, 12*, 118–161.

Braden, L., Finn, C. E., Lerner, L. S., Munroe, S., Petrilli, M. J., Raimi, R. A.,… Stotsky, S. (2000, January). *State of state standards 2000*. Washington, DC: Fordham Foundation.

Brinson, D., & Rhim, L. M. (2009). *Breaking the habit of low performance: Successful school restructuring stories*. Lincoln, IL: Center on Innovation & Improvement.

Brophy, J. (1999). *Teaching*. International Academy of Education Educational Practices Series, H. J. Walberg (Ed.). Geneva, Switzerland: UNESCO, International Bureau of Education. Retrieved from http://www.ibe.unesco.org/en/services/publications/educational-practices.html

Bryk, A. S., Sebring, P. B., Allensworth, E., Luppescu, S., & Easton, J. Q. (2009). *Organizing schools for improvement*. Chicago: University of Chicago Press.

Cameron, J., & Pierce, W. D. (Fall 1994). Reinforcement, reward, and intrinsic motivation: A meta-analysis. *Review of Educational Research, 64*(3), 363–423.

Campbell, J. R., Reese, C. M., O'Sullivan, C., & Dossey, J. A. (1996, November). *NAEP 1994 trends in academic progress*. Washington, DC: National Center for Education Sciences, U.S. Department of Education.

Cannella, G. S., & Reiff, J. C. (1989). Mandating early childhood entrance/retention assessment: Practices in the United States. *Child Study Journal, 19*, 83–99.

Center for Collaborative Education. (2006). *Progress and promise: Results from the Boston pilot schools.* Boston, MA: Author. Retrieved from http://www.ccebos.org/Progress_and_Promise.pdf

Center for Public Education. (2009). *A synthesis of validated research on high performing, high poverty students.* Alexandria, VA: Author. Retrieved from http://www.education.com/reference/article/Ref_Research_review/

Center on Education Policy. (2006). *From the capital to the classroom: Year four of the No Child Left Behind Act.* Washington, DC: Author. Retrieved from http://www.cep-dc.org/_data/global/nidocs/CEP-NCLB-Report-4.pdf

Center on Education Policy. (2007, July). *Moving beyond identification: Assisting schools in improvement.* A report in the series From the Capital to the Classroom: Year 5 of the No Child Left Behind Act. Washington, DC: Author.

Chapple, S., & Richardson, D. (2009). *Doing better for children.* Paris, France: Organization for Economic and Cultural Development.

Christensen, C. M., & Raynor, M. E. (2003). *The innovator's solution: Creating and sustaining successful growth.* Cambridge, MA: Harvard Business School Press.

Collaborative for Academic, Social, & Emotional Learning. (2003). *Safe and sound: An educational guide to evidence-based social and emotional learning (SEL) programs.* Chicago, IL: Author. Retrieved from http://www.casel.org/programs/selecting.php

Coleman, M. R., Buysse, V., & Neitzel, J. (2006). *Recognition and response: An early intervening system for young children at-risk for learning disabilities.* Chapel Hill, NC: University of North Carolina at Chapel Hill, FPG Child Development Institute.

Cooper, H. M. (1989). *Homework.* White Plains, NY: Longman.

Cooper, H. M. (2006). *The battle over homework.* Thousand Oaks, CA: Sage.

Cooper, H. M., Charlton, K., Valentine, J. C., & Muhlenbruck, L. (2000). Making the most of summer school: A meta-analytic and narrative review. *Monographs of the Society for Research in Child Development (Serial No. 260), 65*(1), 1–118.

Cooper, H., Robinson, J., & Patall, E. A. (2006). Does homework improve academic achievement? A synthesis of research, 1987–2003. *Review of Educational Research, 76*(1), 1–62.

Cronin, J., Dahlin, M., Adkins, D., & Kingsbury, G. G. (2007, October). *The proficiency illusion.* Washington, DC: Fordham Institute & Northwest Evaluation Association.

Currie, J. (2001). Early childhood programs. *Journal of Economic Perspectives, 15,* 213–238.

Dailey, D., Fleischman, S., Gil, L., Holtzman, D., O'Day, J., & Vosmer, C. (2005). *Toward more effective school districts: A review of the knowledge base.* Washington, DC: American Institutes for Research. Retrieved from http://www.air.org/projects/Toward%20More%20Effective%20Scchool%20Districts-A%20Review%20of%20the%20Knowledge%20Base%206-14-05%20313%20pm.pdf

David, J., Kannapel, P., & McDiarmid, G. W. (2000). *The influence of distinguished educators on school improvement: A study of Kentucky's school intervention program.* Lexington, KY: Partnership for Kentucky Schools.

Deno, S. (1985). Curriculum-based measurement: The emerging alternative. *Exceptional Children, 52,* 219–232.

Deno, S., & Mirkin, P. (1977). *Data-based program modification.* Minneapolis, MN: Leadership Training Institute for Special Education.

DiBiase, R. W. (2005). *ECS policy brief: State involvement in school restructuring under No Child Left Behind in the 2004–2005 school year.* Denver, CO: Education Commission of the States. Retrieved from http://www.ecs.org/clearinghouse/64/28/6428.pdf

Education Commission of the States. (2007). *School choice state laws: 50 state profiles.* Retrieved from http://www.ecs.org/ecsmain.asp?page=/html/educationIssues/Choice/ChoiceDB_intro.asp

Education Evolving. (2005, July). *Response to intervention: An alternative to traditional eligibility criteria for students with disabilities.* St. Paul, MN: The Center for Policy Studies & Hamline University. Retrieved from http://www.educationevolving.org/pdf/Response_to_Intervention.pdf

Education Testing Service. (2005). *Ready for the real world? Americans speak on high school reform.* Princeton, NJ: Author. Retrieved from http://www.ets.org/Media/Education_Topics/pdf/2005highschoolreform.pdf

Elbaum, B., Vaughn, S., Hughes, M. T., & Moody, S. W. (2000). How effective are one-on-one tutoring programs in reading for elementary students at risk for reading failure? A meta-analysis of the intervention research. *Journal of Educational Psychology, 92*(4), 605–619.

Elias, M. J. (2003). *Academic and social emotional learning.* International Academy of Education Educational Practices Series, H. J. Walberg (Ed.). Geneva, Switzerland: UNESCO, International Bureau of Education. Retrieved from http://www.ibe.unesco.org/en/services/publications/educational-practices.html

Elias, M. J., Tobias, S. E., & Friedlander, B. S. (2000). *Emotionally intelligent parenting: How to raise a self-disciplined, responsible, socially skilled child.* New York: NY: Three Rivers Press.

English, C., & Bareta, L. (2006). *Literacy professional development milestone report.* Wellington, New Zealand: Learning Media.

Entwisle, D. R., & Alexander, K. L. (1993). Entry into school: The beginning school transition and educational stratification in the United States. *Annual Review of Sociology, 19,* 401–423.

Espin, C., & Wallace, T. (2004). *Research institute for progress monitoring.* Minneapolis, MN: University of Minnesota.

Figlio, D., & Kenny, L. (2007, June). Individual teacher incentives and student performance. *Journal of Public Economics, 91*(5), 901–914.

Ericsson, K. A. (2007). Deliberate practice and the modifiability of body and mind: Toward a science of the structure and acquisition of expert and elite performance. *International Journal of Sport Psychology, 38,* 4–34.

Finn, C. E., Petrilli, M. J., & Julian, L. (2006, August). *The state of state standards 2006.* Washington, DC: Fordham Foundation.

Frederick, W. C. (1993). *Extending and intensifying learning time.* Washington, DC: U.S. Department of Education.

Fuchs, D., & Fuchs, L. S. (2006, Jan/Feb/Mar). Introduction to response to intervention: What, why, and how valid is it? *Reading Research Quarterly, 41*(1), 93–99.

Glazerman, S., Tuttle, C., & Baxter, G. (2006, June). *School principals' perspectives on the Passport to Teaching* (MPR No. 6215–400). Washington, DC: Mathematica Policy Research.

Goldring, E., Porter, A. C., Murphy, J., Elliott, S. N., & Cravens, X. (2007, March). *Assessment learning-centered leadership: Connections to research, professional standards, and current practice.* New York, NY: Wallace Foundation.

Gonring, P., Teske, P., & Jupp, B. (2007). *Pay-for-performance teacher compensation: An inside view of Denver's ProComp plan.* Cambridge, MA: Harvard Education Press.

Grigg, W., Donahue, P., & Dion, G. (2007, February). *The Nation's Report Card: 12th-Grade reading and mathematics 2005* (NCES 2007-468). U.S. Department of Education, National Center for Education Statistics. Washington, DC: U.S. Government Printing Office. Retrieved from http://nces.ed.gov/nationsreportcard/pubs/main2005/2007468.asp

Grissmer, D. W., & Flanagan, A. (1998, November). *Exploring rapid achievement gains in North Carolina and Texas.* Washington, DC: National Education Goals Panel.

Grissmer, D. W., & Flanagan, A. (2001). *Searching for indirect evidence for the effects of statewide reforms.* Brookings Papers on Education Policy, 181–229. Washington, DC: Brookings Institution.

Grouws, D. A., & Cebulla, K. J. (2000). *Improving student achievement in mathematics.* International Academy of Education Educational Practices Series, H. J. Walberg (Ed.). Geneva, Switzerland: UNESCO, International Bureau of Education. Retrieved from http://www.ibe.unesco.org/en/services/publications/educational-practices.html

Hanushek, E. A. (1997, Summer). Assessing the effects of school resources on student performance: An update. *Educational Evaluation and Policy Analysis, 19*(2), 141–164.

Hart Research Associates & Public Opinion Strategies. (2005, February). *Rising to the challenge: Are high school graduates ready for college & work? Key findings from surveys among public high school graduates, college instructors, and employers.* Washington, DC: Author. Retrieved from http://www.achieve.org/files/pollreport_0.pdf

Hart, B., & Risley, T. R. (1995). *Meaningful differences in the everyday experience of young American children.* Baltimore: Paul H. Brooks.

Hassel, B. C., & Hassel, E. A. (2007). *Improving teaching through pay for contribution.* Washington, DC: National Governors Association Center for Best Practices.

Hassel, B. C., Hassel, E. A., & Rhim, L. M. (2007). Overview of restructuring. In H. J. Walberg, (Ed.), *Handbook on restructuring and substantial school improvement* (pp. 1-14). Charlotte, NC: Information Age Publishing. Retrieved from http://www.centerii.org/survey/

Hattie, J. A. C. (2009). *Visible learning: A synthesis over 800 meta-analyses relating to achievement.* New York, NY: Routledge.

Herman, R., Dawson, P., Dee, T., Greene, J., Maynard, R., Redding, S., & Darwin, M. (2008). *Turning around chronically low-performing schools: A practice guide* (NCEE #2008-4020). Washington, DC: National Center for Education Evaluation & Regional Assistance, Institute of Education Sciences, U.S. Department of Education. Retrieved from http://ies.ed.gov/ncee/wwc/pdf/practiceguides/Turnaround_pg_04181.pdf

Hirsch, E. D. (1987). *Cultural literacy: What every American needs to know.* Boston: Houghton Mifflin.

Hirsch, E. D. (1998). *What your first grader needs to know.* New York, NY: Delta.

Hirsch, E. D. (1996). *The schools we need and why we don't have them.* New York, NY: Doubleday.

Howell, W. G, West, M. R., & Peterson, P. E. (2008, Fall). The 2008 Education Next Survey-PEPG Survey of Public Opinion. *Education Next, 8*(4). Retrieved from http://educationnext.org/the-2008-education-nextpepg-survey-of-public-opinion/

Hoxby, C. M. (2002). The cost of accountability. In W. M. Evers & H. J. Walberg (Eds.), *School accountability* (pp. 47–74). Stanford, CA: Hoover Institution Press.

Hoxby, C. M., Murarka, S., & Kang, S. (2009). *How New York City's charter schools affect achievement.* Cambridge, MA: New York City Charter Schools Evaluation Project. Retrieved from http://www.nber.org/~schools/charterschoolseval/how_NYC_charter_schools_affect_achievement_sept2009.pdf

Hudgins, K. (2003, May). *Kick start for college: Advanced Placement program proves it pays to study hard.* Fiscal Notes. Austin, TX: Texas Comptroller of Public Accounts, Carole Keeton Strayhorn.

Izumi, L. (2008). *What works: Inside model charter schools.* Lincoln, IL: Center on Innovation & Improvement. Retrieved from http://www.centerii.org/techassist/solutionfinding/resources/Izumi%20final%20ref%20editedApril%202007.pdf

Jackson, C. K. (2008, Fall). Cash for test scores: The impact of the Texas Advanced Placement Incentive Program. *Education Next,* 71–76. Retrieved from http://works.bepress.com/c_kirabo_jackson/10

Jerald, C. D. (2001). *Dispelling the myth revisited.* Washington, DC: Education Trust.

Judd, E. L., Tan, L., & Walberg, H. J. (2001). *Teaching additional languages.* International Academy of Education Educational Practices Series, H. J. Walberg (Ed.). Geneva, Switzerland: UNESCO, International Bureau of Education. Retrieved from http://www.ibe.unesco.org/en/services/publications/educational-practices.html

Kanter, R. M. (1991, May–June). Transcending business boundaries: 12,000 world managers view change. *Harvard Business Review,* 151–164.

Kaplan, S. N., Klebanov, M. M., & Sorensen, M. (2008, July). *Which CEO characteristics and abilities matter?* Stockholm, Sweden: Swedish Institute for Financial Research. Retrieved from http://papers.ssrn.com/sol3/papers.cfm?abstract_id=972446

Karoly, L. A., Greenwood, P. W., Everingham, S. S., Houbé, J., Kilburn, M. R., Rydell, C. P.,...Chiesa, J. (1998). *Investing in our children: What we know and don't know about the costs and benefits of early childhood interventions.* Santa Monica, CA: RAND.

Kowal, J., Rosch, J. L., Hassel, E. A., & Hassel, B. C. (2009). *Performance-based dismissals: Cross-sector lessons for school turnarounds.* Lincoln, IL: Center on Innovation & Improvement.

Kremer, M., Miguel, E., & Thornton, R. (2007, January). *Incentives to learn* (Unpublished manuscript). Cambridge, MA: Harvard University.

Kulik, J. A. (2001). *Effectiveness of instructional technology in elementary and secondary schools: What does the research say?* Ann Arbor, MI: University of Michigan.

Kuper, S. (2009, September 12). Action man. *Financial Times,* 19.

LaParo, K. M., & Pianta, R. C. (2000, Winter). Predicting children's competence in the early school years: A meta-analytic review. *Review of Educational Research, 70*(4), 443–484.

Larson, R. (2001). How U.S. children and adolescents spend time. *Current Directions in Psychological Science, 10*(5), 160–164.

Lauer, P. A., Akiba, M., Wilkerson, S. B., Apthorp, H. S., Snow, D., & Martin-Glenn, M. L. (2006). Out-of-school-time programs: A meta-analysis of effects for at-risk students. *Review of Educational Research, 76*(2), 275–313.

Lazear, E. P., & Shaw, K. L. (2007). *Personnel economics.* Cambridge, MA: National Bureau of Economic Research.

Le Floch, K. C., Taylor, J., & Zhang, Y. (2006). *Schools in NCLB restructuring: National trends.* Washington, DC: American Institutes for Research.

Lock, E. A., Shaw, K. N., Saari, L. M., & Latham, G. P. (1981). Goal setting and task performance. *Psychological Bulletin, 90*, 125–152.

Marzano, R. J. (2000). *A new era of school reform: Going where the research takes us.* Aurora, CO: Mid-Continent Research for Education and Learning.

Marzano, R. J. (2004). *Building background knowledge for academic achievement.* Washington, DC: Association for Supervision and Curriculum Development.

Mathematica Policy Research. (2002). *Early Head Start: Making a difference in the lives of infants and toddlers and their families: The impacts of Early Head Start.* Princeton, NJ: Author.

Mattingly, D. J., Prislin, R., McKenzie, T. L., Rodriguez, J. L., & Kayzar, B. (2002). Evaluating evaluations: The case of parent involvement programs. *Review of Educational Research, 72*(1), 549–576.

Mazzeo, C., & Berman, I. (2003). *Reaching new heights: Turning around low-performing schools.* Washington, DC: National Governor's Association, Center for Best Practices.

McNeil, M. (2007, February 13). Utah Gov. signs broad voucher law. *Education Week.* Retrieved from http://www.edweek.org/ew/articles/2007/02/13/23utah_webupdate.h26.html

Meisels, S. J. (1999). Assessing readiness. In R. C. Pianta & M. Cox (Eds.), *The transition to kindergarten: Research, policy, training, and practice.* Baltimore: Paul H. Brookes.

Michigan Department of Education. (n.d.). *MI-MAP.* Lansing, MI: Author. Retrieved from http://www.michigan.gov/mde/0,1607,7-140-28753_33424—,00.html,

Milken, M. (2009, October 5). Prosperity rests on human and social capital. *Financial Times,* 13.

Moore, M. G., & Anderson, W. G. (2003). *Handbook of distance education.* Mahwah, NJ: Lawrence Erlbaum.

National Center for Education Statistics. (2007). *Nation's Report Card.* Washington, DC: Author. Retrieved from http://nces.ed.gov/nationsreportcard/

Nelson, S. (2008, February 28). *Performance-based pay in the federal government.* Paper presented at the conference, Performance Incentives: Their Growing Impact on American K–12 Education, Vanderbilt University, Nashville, TN.

North American Council for Online Teaching. (2008). *National standards for quality online teaching.* Vienna, VA: Author. Retrieved from http://www.inacol.org/resources/nationalstandards/NACOL%20Standards%20Quality%20Online%20 Teaching.pdf

Palaich, R. M., Griffin, D., & van der Ploeg, A. (2004). *State education data systems that increase learning and improve accountability.* Naperville, IL: Learning Point Associates.

Pang, E. S., Muaka, A., Bernhardt, E. B., & Kamil, M. L. (2003). *Teaching reading.* International Academy of Education Educational Practices Series, H. J. Walberg (Ed.). Geneva, Switzerland: UNESCO, International Bureau of Education. Retrieved from http://www.ibe.unesco.org/en/services/publications/educational-practices.html

Pascale, R., Millemann, M., & Gioja, L. (1997). Changing the way we change. *Harvard Business Review, 75*(6), 126–139.

Pashler, H., Bain, P., Bottge, B., Graesser, A., Koedinger, K., McDanield, M., & Metcalfe, J. (2007). *Organizing instruction and study to improve learning* (NCER 2007–2004). Washington, DC: National Center for Education Research, Institute of Education Sciences, U.S. Department of Education. Retrieved from: http://ies.ed.gov/ncer/pubs/practiceguides/20072004.asp

Phillips, G. E., McNaughton, S., & MacDonald, S. (2001). *Picking up the pace: Effective literacy interventions for accelerated progress over the transition into decile one schools* (Final Report). Wellington, New Zealand: Ministry of Education.

Podgursky, M. J., & Springer, M. G. (2007). Teacher performance pay. *Journal of Policy Analysis and Management, 26*(4), 909–949.

Pomerantz, E. M., Moorman, E. A., & Litwack, S. D. (2007). The how, whom, and why of parents' involvement in children's academic lives: More is not always better. *Review of Educational Research, 9*(77), 373–410.

Public Impact. (2007). *School turnarounds: A review of the cross-sector evidence on dramatic organizational improvement.* Lincoln, IL: Center on Innovation & Improvement. Retrieved from http://www.centerii.org/survey/

Quality counts 2008. (January 10, 2008). *Education Week.* Bethesda, MD: Editorial Projects in Education.

Ravitch, D. (2001). Introduction. In D. Ravitch (Ed.), *Brookings papers on education policy, 2001* (pp. 1–8). Washington, DC: Brookings Institution.

Redding, S. (2000). *Parents and learning.* International Academy of Education Educational Practices Series, H. J. Walberg (Ed.). Geneva, Switzerland: UNESCO, International Bureau of Education. Retrieved from http://www.ibe.unesco.org/en/services/publications/educational-practices.html

Redding, S., & Walberg, H. J. (Eds.). (2007). *Handbook on statewide systems of support.* Charlotte, NC: Information Age Publishing. Retrieved from http://www.centerii.org/survey/

Reichardt, R. (2002). *Recruiting and retaining teachers with alternative pay.* Aurora, CO: Mid-Continent Research for Education and Learning.

Reville, P. (2004). *Examining state intervention capacity: How can the state better support low performing schools and districts?* Boston, MA: Rennie Center for Education Research & Policy.

Reynolds, A. J. (2000). *Success in early intervention: The Chicago Child–Parent Centers.* Lincoln, NE: University of Nebraska Press.

Reynolds, A. J., Temple, J. A., Robertson, D. L., & Mann, E. L. (2001). Long-term effects of an early childhood intervention on educational achievement and juvenile arrest: A 15 year follow-up of low-income children in public schools. *Journal of the American Medical Association, 285*, 2339–2346.

Rhim, L. M., Hassel, B., & Redding, S. (2007). State role in supporting school improvement. In S. Redding & H. J. Walberg (Eds.), *Handbook on statewide systems of support*. Lincoln, IL: Center on Innovation and Improvement.

Scott, C., Kober, N., Rentner, D. S., & Jennings, J. (2006). *Wrestling the devil in the details: An early look at restructuring in California*. Washington, DC: Center on Education Policy.

Scott-Little, C., Hamann, M. S., & Jurs, S. G. (2002). Evaluations of after-school programs: A meta-evaluation of methodologies and narrative synthesis of findings. *American Journal of Evaluation, 23*(4), 387–419.

Shih, C., & Weekly, D. E. (2005). *Using new media*. International Academy of Education Educational Practices Series, H. J. Walberg (Ed.). Geneva, Switzerland: UNESCO, International Bureau of Education. Retrieved from http://www.ibe.unesco.org/en/services/publications/educational-practices.html

Simon, H. A. (1981). *Sciences of the artificial*. Cambridge, MA: MIT Press.

Spira, J. B. (2009). *Managing the knowledge workforce*. New York, NY: BaseX.

Stanovich, K. E. (1986). Matthew effects in reading. *Reading Research Quarterly, 21*, 360–406.

Staver, J. R. (2007). *Teaching science*. International Academy of Education Educational Practices Series, H. J. Walberg (Ed.). Geneva, Switzerland: UNESCO, International Bureau of Education. Retrieved from http://www.ibe.unesco.org/en/services/publications/educational-practices.html

Steiner, L. (2009). *Tough decisions: Closing persistently low-performing schools*. Lincoln, IL.: Center on Innovation & Improvement. Retrieved from http://www.centerii.org/survey/

Sticht, T. G., & James, J. H. (1984). Listening and reading. In P. D. Pearson, R. Barr, M. Kamil, & P. L. Mosenthal (Eds.), *Handbook of reading research* (Vol. 1, pp. 293–317). New York, NY: Longman.

Tarrance Group. (2007, April). *Key findings from a survey of attitudes in the state of Florida*. Retrieved from http://www.abcte.org/files/Florida_Poll.pdf

Timperley, H., Bertanees, C., & Parr, J. (2006). A case study: Promoting teacher learning using a needs analysis approach. In J. Parr, H. Timperley, P. Reddish, R. Jesson, & R. Adams (Eds.), *Literacy professional development project: Identifying effective teaching and professional development practices for enhanced student learning*. Milestone 5 (Final Report). Wellington, New Zealand: Learning Media.

Timperley, H., Wilson, A., Barrar, H., & Fung, I. (2007). *Teacher professional learning and development: Best evidence synthesis iteration*. Wellington, New Zealand: Ministry of Education. Retrieved from http://www.educationcounts.govt.nz/publications/series/2515/15341

U.S. Department of Education, Office of Elementary and Secondary Education. (2006, July). *LEA and school improvement: Non-regulatory guidance* (revised). Washington, DC: Author.

U.S. Department of Education, National Center for Education Statistics. (2007, October). *The condition of education 2007* (NCES 2007-064). Washington, DC: U.S. Government Printing Office.

U.S. Department of Health and Human Services, Administration for Children and Families. (2005, May). *Head Start impact study: First year findings.* Washington, DC: Author. Retrieved from http://www.acf.hhs.gov/programs/opre/hs/impact_study/reports/first_yr_finds/firstyr_finds_authors.html

Velluntino, F. R., Scanlon, D. M., Sipay, E. R., Small, S., Chen, R., Pratt, A., & Denckla, M. B. (1996). Cognitive profiles of difficult-to-remediate and readily remediated poor readers: Early intervention as a vehicle for distinguishing between cognitive and experiential deficits as basic causes of specific reading disability. *Journal of Educational Psychology, 88,* 601–638.

Vosniadou, S. (2001). *How children learn.* International Academy of Education Educational Practices Series, H. J. Walberg (Ed.). Geneva, Switzerland: UNESCO, International Bureau of Education. Retrieved from http://www.ibe.unesco.org/en/services/publications/educational-practices.html

Walberg, H. J. (1983). Scientific literacy and economic productivity in international perspective. *Daedalus, 112*(2), 1–28.

Walberg, H. J. (1988). Creativity and talent as learning. In R. Sternberg (Ed.), *The nature of creativity* (pp. 247–372). New York, NY: Cambridge University Press.

Walberg, H. J. (1998, November 4). Incentivized school standards work. *Education Week, 18*(10), 48.

Walberg, H. J. (1998). Uncompetitive American schools: Causes and cures. In D. Ravitch (Ed.), *Brookings papers on education policy 1998* (pp. 173–226). Washington, DC: Brookings Institution Press.

Walberg, H. J. (2001). Achievement in American schools. In T. Moe (Ed.), *A primer on America's schools* (pp. 43–68). Stanford, CA: Hoover Institution Press.

Walberg, H. J. (2006). Improving educational productivity. In R. F. Subotnik & H. J. Walberg (Eds.), *The scientific basis of educational productivity.* Greenwich, CT: Information Age Publishing.

Walberg, H. J. (Ed.). (2007a). *Handbook on restructuring and substantial school improvement.* Charlotte, NC: Information Age Publishing. Retrieved from http://www.centerii.org/survey/

Walberg, H. J. (2007b). *School choice: The findings.* Washington, DC: Cato Institute.

Walberg, H. J. (2010). *Advancing student achievement.* Stanford, CA: Hoover Institution Press.

Walberg, H. J., & Lai, J. S. (1999). Meta-analytic effects for policy. In G. J. Cizek (Ed.), *Handbook of educational policy* (pp. 419–453). San Diego, CA: Academic Press.

Walberg, H. J., & Tsai, S. L. (1984). Matthew effects in education. *American Educational Research Journal, 20,* 359–374.

Wallace, T., Stariha, W. E., & Walberg, H. J. (2004). *Teaching, speaking, listening, and writing.* International Academy of Education Educational Practices Series, H. J. Walberg (Ed.). Geneva, Switzerland: UNESCO, International Bureau of Education. Retrieved from http://www.ibe.unesco.org/en/services/publications/educational-practices.html

Walsh, K., & Tracy, C. O. (2004). *Increasing the odds: How good policies can yield better teachers.* Washington, DC: National Council on Teacher Quality.

Wang, M. C., Haertel, G. D., & Walberg, H. J. (1993). Toward a knowledge base for school learning. *Review of Educational Research, 63*(3), 249–294.

Wayne, A. J., & Youngs, P. (2003). Teacher characteristics and student achievement gains: A review. *Review of Educational Research, 73*(1), 89–122.

Westat. (2006). *Statewide systems of support profiles.* Rockville, MD: Author.

White, K. R. (1985). Efficacy of early intervention. *Journal of Special Education, 19,* 401–416.

Wigfield, A., & Asher, S. R. (1984). Social and motivational influences on reading. In P. D. Pearson, R. Barr, M. Kamil, & P. L. Mosenthal (Eds.), *Handbook of reading research* (Vol. 1, pp. 423–452). New York, NY: Longman.

Woessmann, L. (2001, Summer). Why students in some countries do better. *Education Matters,* 65–74.

Yinger, J., Bloom, H. S., Borch-Supan, A., & Ladd, H. F. (1988). *Property taxes and housing values.* Boston: Academic Press.

ABOUT THE AUTHOR

Herbert J. Walberg began his education career as a regularly certified teacher in the Chicago Public Schools and later served as a professor at Harvard and the University of Illinois at Chicago after earning a Ph.D. in educational psychology at the University of Chicago. He is now Distinguished Visiting Fellow at Stanford University and Chief Scientific Advisor to the Center on Innovation & Improvement. He has written and edited more than sixty-five books and written some 350 articles on such topics as educational assessment and effectiveness, and exceptional human accomplishments.

Walberg has given invited lectures in Australia, Belgium, China, England, France, Germany, Israel, Italy, Japan, the Netherlands, South Africa, Sweden, Taiwan, the United States, and Venezuela to educators, psychologists, and policy makers. He has frequently testified before congressional committees, state legislators, and federal courts. He is the only American to have served on the National Assessment Governing Board and the presidentially-appointed National Board for Educational Sciences.

For the National Science Foundation, he carried out comparative research in Japanese and American schools. For the U.S. Department of State and the White House, he organized a radio series and edited a book about American education distributed in seventy-four countries. He edits for the Geneva-based United Nations International Bureau of Education a booklet

Improving Student Learning: Action Principles for Families, Classrooms, Schools, Districts, and States, pages 139–140
 139

series on education practices that is distributed in more than one hundred countries.

Walberg chaired the Organization for Economic Cooperation and Development's Scientific Advisory Group on education indicators and advised the United Nations Educational Scientific, and Cultural Organization and government officials in Israel, Italy, Japan, Singapore, Sweden, and the United Kingdom on education research and policy. He has served on seven boards, including that of the California-based Foundation for Teaching Economics. He chairs the boards of the Beck Foundation that fosters children's literacy and the Heartland Institute that synthesizes policy research from more than 300 think tanks for elected government officials.

Breinigsville, PA USA
21 December 2010
251931BV00003B/1/P